THE DISTANT SCENE

The author writes:

'Our villagers then led a simple life. The
land was worked by simple tackle. This was
an age when carters walked with a rolling
gait with their ash plants on summer
Sundays, as if following the plough, when
boys of thirteen drove three-horse teams,
drawing huge loads of hay through ten-foot
gateways on farm waggons. This was a
stay-at-home world. The village was really
alive on spring evenings. Not with motor
cars but children with hoops and tops,
then later on cricket in the rickyards, rick
pegs for stumps, the hayrick as wicket-
keeper. Children would walk a mile to the
main road to meet the steam-roller.'

The
Distant Scene

Fred Archer

CORONET BOOKS
Hodder Paperbacks Ltd., London

Copyright © 1967 by Fred Archer
First published by
Hodder and Stoughton Ltd. 1967
Coronet edition 1973
Second impression 1973
Third impression 1974

Acknowledgment is due to Sidgwick &
Jackson Ltd for permission to quote the
poem on p. 138 by John Drinkwater.

Printed in Great Britain
for Coronet Books, Hodder Paperbacks Ltd.,
St. Paul's House, Warwick Lane, EC4P 4AH,
by Richard Clay (The Chaucer Press), Ltd.,
Bungay, Suffolk.

ISBN 0 340 17863 9

A letter to the author from
JOHN MOORE

Dear Mr. Archer,

I read your typescript last night and was really delighted by it. The style is just right; it is absolutely genuine and some of the stories are extremely funny. For instance I loved the chap looking up at his first aeroplane and saying, 'Unt 'e up a depth?', and some of the reminiscences about Blenheim and that story about Farley's donkey. The writing is beautifully fresh ('I wasn't in a position to argue with men who had seen almost as many leap years as I had seen Christmas Days'). I do warmly congratulate you.

Yours sincerely,
John Moore

AUTHOR'S PREFACE

I HAVE BEEN asked by all sorts of people, 'Why have you, a farmer, written a book?' All of us are aware of the change in village life that has happened within living memory. It is put very aptly in the following words:

'We die my friend. Not we alone, but that which each man loved, and prized in his peculiar nook of earth, dies with him or is changed.'

When the village was a compact unit with its blacksmith, wheelwright, baker, shoemaker, ladder and hurdle maker, doctor, all these people had their own characteristics. They were all different, all had a different story.

I felt that it would be such a pity that when these characters died their sayings, their customs, their ways of life and the way they dressed, should go with them.

Much of the material in this book I have gleaned from relatives and friends; some from personal experience.

My main object had been to give a faithful and sincere record of life and events in our village from about 1876 until 1939.

As a native of this plot under the hill I felt in such close contact with the people over the years, listening to their tales. Having made time just to stand and stare.

When I started to write it seemed to be in my being. It just came.

Hoping it's different and you enjoy it. I enjoyed writing it.

LIST OF ILLUSTRATIONS

Between pages 80 and 81

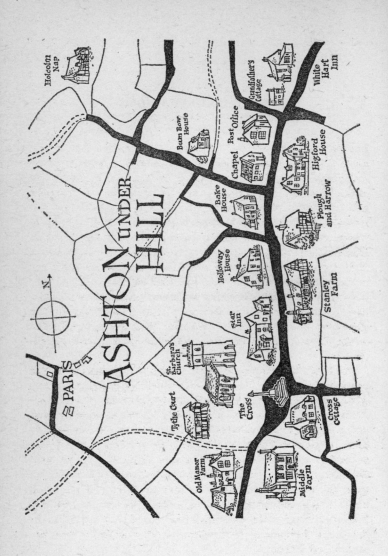

PARIS

ASHTON UNDER HILL

Holcolm Nap

Bum Baw House

Post Office

Chapel

Grandfather's Cottage

White Hart Inn

Higford House

Plough and Harrow

Bake House

Holloway House

Stanley Farm

Star Inn

St. Barbara's Church

The Cross

Cross Cottage

Tythe Court

Old Manor Farm

Middle Farm

N

CHAPTER ONE

THE VILLAGE UNDER THE HILL

IN A WORLD of change the few things in our village that remain are the black and white half-timbered houses, the ancient oaks in Church Close, the moat, which is really the fish-pond of an earlier moat, and the village street which runs due north up the hill. On a cold, crisp winter's night, the Pole Star and Jack and his Waggon—the Plough—stand sentinel, pointing the way to Townsend, where the road starts on its snaky way towards Elmley Castle. A fifteenth-century cross stands at the entrance to the churchyard. Its stone steps have been worn down by politicians, preachers, little children and old men resting their weary limbs, smoking their clay pipes and talking of even earlier days. The Men's Friendly Society (the Sick and Dividend Club started by Thomas Packer in 1876) had their photographs taken on the village cross; so did the school children and their school-teachers.

Life in the last century was grim for the labouring classes, this being a poor parish. The roads were half their present width, with deep wheel-ruts. Stones off Bredon Hill and a soft lime-stone from Holcombe Nap were used to fill these in. Water was drawn from numerous wells and the Cross end of the village drew its supplies from a stone half-pipe still there, jutting out of the hill. No drain ran down our road in those days; an open ditch where ducks swam and boys paddled ran sweet and clean from the source on Spring Hill past the Sheep Wash Pool, Shaw Green and down the village. Many of the cottages had little bridges to cross the stream which varied from a quiet amb-ling ripple in summer to a raging torrent down into the Car-rants Brook in winter.

The squire and parson ruled supreme and saw to it that everyone kept their proper station in life. Boys leaving school had but one job waiting for them—plough-driving a team of four heavy shires pulling a single furrow through the heavy loam and clay of the parish. The girls who didn't go into domestic service locally often went to the larger houses of Cheltenham, starting on the bottom rung of the ladder. What was there for the labourer to look forward to apart from Club Day on the Wednesday after Whitsun and a visit to Evesham Mop and a pair of new boots in October paid for out of the little extra harvesting money? No wonder old Oliver, a rough carpenter, used to say the day after Ashton Club, 'It's only eleven months two weeks and a fortnight to next club day.'

But Dick Miles rode his penny-farthing bike one hundred miles to London, came back and told the natives that there was a man up there who knew everything. Beckford was always the senior partner of our villages and the original squire came from there. The Hall was lit by gas and any Ashtonian who knew a bit more than the rest was told, 'Oi, thee 'ast bin to Beckford.' The milk produced at Beckford was made into butter and cheese and taken to Evesham by carriers' cart.

The younger men tired of low wages and the rule of the squire and left the village for the iron foundries of the Black Country and to work on what they called 'the rail road'. Some were more venturesome and emigrated to Canada. So parochial was the mind of the older villagers that one enquired, 'Where is this Canada? Anywhere in England?' When he was told it was way out west he said, 'Oh oi, I knows—Wales road.' The villagers—I fancy because of intermarriage, one generation after another—were like the rooks; if a lover brought home a foreign bride the pair were forced to build in a distant tree, the sentiment being, 'If Jacob take a wife of the daughters of Heth, what good shall my life do me? Geography was not a strong point with the old villagers who didn't like to travel so far that the beech trees dominating Bredon on Great Hill were out of sight. But as they supped their pints in the White Hart they had an excellent view of Broadway Tower, and Avon Perry, who boasted about his far-seeing eyes, declared he could see a fly on Broddy Monument about six miles away. Not to be beaten, old

Oliver said, 'Oi, and I a just sin him wink his eye, and them two tots on the mantelpiece in the bar be just alike, especially that one.'

There was little organised entertainment in the late nineteenth century but there is no doubt that our village, like others, had a few of the driest natural humorists. Their presence made life bearable.

CHAPTER TWO

SQUIRE BOSWORTH AND UNCLE JIM

UNCLE JIM was ten when he left school. This was in 1882, and he had passed what was then known as 'the Grand Standard', Standard four.

He started his working life crow-minding for Squire Bosworth at sixpence per day. His job was to keep the crows off the Squire's corn, walking from field to field and shouting himself hoarse. The Squire then made him a ploughboy, working with Jarvy Hill. Uncle Jim had four massive shire horses in his charge which he drove up and down the furrows, ploughing one furrow at a time, with Jarvy holding the plough tails and talking to the horses in a language not yet familiar to Uncle Jim. 'Het' meant push the team off to the right. 'How' or 'Waa' was the signal to keep them a little to the left. 'On the headland' or 'addledum' as the locals called it, was really the turning place of the team under the hedge. To 'turn jig' was to turn right and 'come agun' or 'come again' was turn left. 'Jig agun', 'come agun', 'come 'ee back', Jarvy would shout. This sort of thing was soon picked up by the ploughboys from each other, but some carters were hard and if the furrow didn't finish straight thought nothing of throwing a clat or clod of clay at the boy or giving him a stroke with the whip. The whips were carried by the ploughboy and were made to crack rather than to strike the horses with. With a short piece of whip cord joined to the end of the plaited leather whip, it could be cracked almost like the ringmaster's at a circus.

Uncle Jim was lucky in his ploughman, for Jarvy was a meek and mild man. Some termed him 'a bit sawny'. His movements were slow as he reeled behind the plough which bit into the clay and when Uncle Jim asked to hold the plough tails for a while, Jarvy would say, 'All righ' then, Jimmy me byoy, but keep thee eyes open cos if he ketches us what ull the maaster say?' So Uncle Jim learned to plough with four horses and Jarvy drove them dressed as he was, corduroy trousers, yorks (straps) below the knee, a Derby tweed jacket with a poacher's pocket inside big enough to hold two rabbits, a coloured muffler round his neck and a billycock hat green with age crowning a weather-beaten old face.

Uncle Jim was now getting sevenpence a day and an occasional rabbit which he and Jarvy would snare, or kill with the plough paddle, a little spade carried to clean the plough. As the team moved up and down the ground a rabbit would be squatting in a form in a rougher part of the stubble and a blow with the paddle secured a dinner for one of them, Jarvy or Jim. The dead rabbit was hocked, paunched and hung on the hames of the foremost horse until they reached the headland, then put safely inside the frail (food basket) hanging on the hedge with bait inside for man and boy. When the teams set out at seven in the morning two wooden bottles or costrels full of cider were hung on the hames by a little handle; Jarvy's held half a gallon and Jim's a quart. This was known as the 'lowance, poured out of a barrel every morning by Betsy Bradfield, one of the Squire's housemaids at the Manor. The quantity of free cider was doubled for harvest, haymaking and threshing being particularly dry and dusty jobs. Nailus the shepherd used to drink his half-gallon straight up and filled his bottle with spring water on his way round his flock on Bredon Hill.

After a time Uncle Jim learned that the other ploughboys on the farm were getting eightpence a day so he asked the Squire for eightpence, the same as the others. The Squire replied, 'Ah, but they be bigger than what thee bist. Thee bisn't tall enough to hear the clock strike.' So Uncle Jim left the Squire and went blackberry-picking on Bredon Hill. This was a great success. He walked cross-country about five miles to Evesham, came back on the train and had two shillings left from his sale of the fruit after he had paid his fare on the homeward journey. But who should he meet on the train but the Squire himself, who told

Uncle Jim that he was going towards prison as fast as he could go.

Uncle Jim then went to work for old Harry Burford, milking, butter-making and helping the housekeeper with the hens and pigs. Now Harry Burford was apt to get 'market peart' and got home very late some winter nights, but his cob, Blackbird, brought him safely to Bum Bow where his small farm was. Uncle stayed with the housekeeper to stable the horse safely when Master Burford arrived. Harry Burford was always buying litters, or 'bellies' as he called them, of eight-week-old pigs and making porkers of them by feeding them on skim milk, boiled linseed and sharps. He bought one lot at Beckford and Uncle Jim told him he didn't like the look of them, they looked scruffy. Sure enough they had swine fever and had to be killed and buried in lime. No doubt Harry Burford's judgment had been impaired at the inn. As Uncle Jim said, 'He was a good man round a barrel but no cooper.'

Meanwhile Squire Bosworth was becoming more and more eccentric, not an uncommon thing among squires because of intermarriage. Harry Burford's misfortune with the 'belly' of pigs from Beckford was common knowledge and Squire Bosworth said he knew a way of preventing pigs from getting this disease: cut a little bit off the ears and tail of each pig. The next Monday morning he arranged to meet George Bradfield, a cowman and pigman, in the stable of Middle Farm House. The Squire arrived complete with butcher's apron, carving knife and steel hanging from his belt. 'Catch the first pig, George.' George, who had already got them in close quarters in the loosebox of the stable, obeyed and skilfully handed the first weaner pig to the Squire, who cut off half its ears and half its tail. After three pigs had been treated, George said in a trembling voice, 'I 'udn't cut quite so much off if I was you, gaffer.' The Squire was in no mood to listen to George. 'Shut thee mouth,' he said, 'or I'll serve thee the same.' What could George do? As he told me, the Squire was savage as a tup, and despite the blood they did several more pigs before he called it a day.

One morning that same winter when, as old George Bradfield

said, 'it was a-freezing you just like big guns', they had been
threshing wheat for a few days and the Squire was out in the
rickyard with his apron over his breeches and his pigskin gaiters
just showing. He was a slightly built man who slouched rather
than walked. 'George,' he shouted, 'these dogs be starved to
death a cold. Give um some cider.' He kept a mixed pack,
mainly lurchers. George took them one by one, pouring some of
his precious half-gallon into a cider horn and into each dog's
mouth, with most of it running out the other side. 'What about
Brindy? Thee bist frightened of him?' 'I be,' said George, 'and
it's taking all my cider.' 'Never mind,' said the Squire, 'there is
plenty more in the barn.' He had a good supply there and one
barrel held five hogsheads.

By this time Harry Burford had retired and Uncle Jim got a
job with the squire again. This time it was cleaning out Carrants Brook. He was working down in Didcot Ham with a man
named Stevens, shovelling out the mud. They caught a number
of eels and trout in the brook and took them to the Squire, who
put them in the moat. One day the Squire, who was now getting dangerous with his gun, levelled it at them saying, 'I
thought your hats were two black crows.'

As Uncle Jim was going by one dinner time, the Squire stopped him and asked if he had noticed the ducks feeding with the
hens on the tail corn in the rickyard. The ducks were shovelling
up the corn and the hens picking it up. 'It's not fair, you know.
Catch the ducks.' Stevens had arrived by then and helped Jim
get them into the duck-pen. The Squire, believe it or not, took
out his penknife, sharpened the beaks of the ducks and said,
'There, fair's fair. Peck up your corn like the hens.'

He was accused by some of being cruel to his animals, so to
prove his stock was well cared for, he held a show up in the Big
Seeds where trotting races and horse-jumping took place. All
his stock was penned up there; the older men were sent up into
the big wood to cut nut sticks to walk around the animals and
look important. Barrels of beer and cider and joints of beef were
shared by all and sundry. The Squire cut up postcards and gave
everybody a piece which entitled them to one drink. Of course

these were used time and time again. The animals were, as old George said, 'as full as blowed ticks and as round as apple dumplings.' The Squire said he'd showed people whether he was cruel to animals. His show is still talked of today by just a few who remember.

George Bradfield and Uncle Jim were always concerned when the Squire went to market. He developed a passion for buying bulls and sometimes let them out of their pens at Manor Farm into an open yard to watch them fight. One white shorthorn became very savage. Apart from the plough teams, he had lots of horses roaming Bredon Hill; they were eight or nine years old, had never been broken in and never had a collar on. As George remarked to Uncle Jim, 'Jim, me lad, when fools be born they got to be kept.'

One day the Squire thought he would straighten Back Lane, which joins the A435. He took all his men with picks and shovels down this most crooked lane, stood on the main road and with his gun at the ready threatened to shoot any man who went more than a yard out of straight. He had become so trigger happy that the shot had been taken out of his cartridges for everyone's peace of mind. About two hundred yards of Back Lane runs straight to this day, then comes a left-angled bend where I presume the project was called off.

His keenness on shooting showed itself in other ways. He took to shooting at night, and if any of his men didn't answer a knock at the door he would shoot at the bedroom window. He used to ask Uncle Jim, 'Didst thee hear me shoot last night?' Uncle Jim would say, 'No, sir.' 'If ever thee hears me shoot, thee get up. I shall be wanting somebody.' When old George heard the Squire shooting, he would say, 'Thur's another barrel empty and I ant had a spot.' Yes, old George, he was a great character. When the first aeroplane came over, he said, 'My goy, unt he up a depth.'

The Squire now bought himself two steam-ploughing engines and yet another steam engine for threshing or wood sawing, doing away with the old saw pit behind the bull-pen. He called these engines his black hosses and used to fetch away two or three of the bigger boys from the village school to help him clean the brasses on them. They were polished till, as Uncle Jim said, 'you could a sin to shave be looking at the shining brass'.

The young men had stopped working for the Squire except Stevens, Uncle Jim and a few more, but the old men still came to work, some on two sticks, crippled by age or rheumatics. The Squire was quite fair about this. 'I have had the best out of you and I'll have the worst,' he said. Threshing time came round and Stevens and Uncle Jim found themselves two able-bodied men doing most of the work among a gang of sick, lame and lazy. Uncle Jim, now getting nine shillings a week, cider and a breakfast of boiled fat bacon on Sundays for Sunday work, asked the Squire for a rise. 'No, my lad,' he said, 'that's your wage and more than thee bist worth.' But handing Uncle his gun he took one hundred gold sovereigns from his pockets and offered them to him if he would go and shoot the village doctor, who had offended him. A favourite trick of the Squire was to throw these sovereigns in the air to fall on the blue lias stone by his back door and then get old George Bradfield to pick them up and count them.

After the threshing Uncle Jim left the Squire and went to work on 'the rail road'. The Squire himself went into hiding for three years, just occasionally to be seen peeping behind the curtains. He sometimes shot from his bedroom window or up the chimneys at imaginary owls, but there was no lead in his cartridges. Then the rumour went round that the Squire had come out. They were threshing at the Cross Barn, it was bait time and the engine was silent as the men ate their bread and cheese and swilled away some of the inevitable dust with the fermented juice of the fox whelp and black taunton or home-made cider.

'Get them wheels a-turning,' shouted the Squire to Fireman Davis. He gently slid the throttle over and the engine started the belt turning, the machine gathering speed from a low hum to a higher-pitched moan, moan, moan. The Squire was happy. The men continued their lunch. He made a round of his farms and found men in one field burning 'squitch' (couch grass) cleared off the land. 'Don't burn any more,' he said. 'Get the muck-cart

and litter the cow-yard with it. It 'ull make the best of muck.'
They did as they were told. Once more the Squire was giving
out the orders and it pleased him.

But he had his off days and was found one morning sitting in
a wheelbarrow in the middle of the moat. His men waded in
and rescued him, only to be told he was fed up with this country and was off to America. Soon after that, when he was out
riding in his trap with the groom, the Squire collapsed and died.
A blessing, we may say, but in his own fashion he had enjoyed
his unusual life.

CHAPTER THREE

THE BRADFIELDS

GEORGE BRADFIELD had two uncles, John and Sep, Sep being short for Septimus, the seventh child of his parents. John and Sep, apart from their employment as drainers with Mr. Fred Washbourne of Higford House, had a sizeable allotment in Hill Withy. Two bachelors, they lived in a thatched wattle and daub cottage which nestled in a small orchard just below the Little Hill. John and Sep always had a pig in the sty. It was bought in the early summer, named Satan, and killed at about sixteen score the following winter. On their allotment they grew their potatoes, a strip of wheat, some barley for the pig and runner beans. The surplus vegetables were sold to the few retired gentry or given to someone who was in need. They toiled constantly, winter and summer, in winds and dull weather, their dark hair just showing under their pancake caps and their faces brown as a berry. Fred Washbourne said their hands were 'hard as the devil's back tith'. They had by their thrift gained a measure of independence and employed other men to help them drain the heavy clay land belonging to Mr. Washbourne. Draining was done as piece work, or 'by the rip' as George, their nephew, whom I knew well, called it.

Tile draining had not been common for long and John and Sep had often filled in the trenches with ash or gorse faggots tied with withy sticks. Their tools were few but enough to make a good job of their work: a fork to dig the top spit back and a graft or long-tapered spade to dig the subsoil. In clay, eighteen inches was the usual depth, but a fall had to be maintained to the ditch beside the hedge bottom. A cleanser, made of iron shaped like half a pipe set at an acute angle on the end of a long stick, was used to clear the trench bottom of loose crumbs and provide an even channel for the pipes. My grandfather, who also had an allotment in Carrants Field near the Bradfields, helped them at times. Imagine working in mud and water in the winter-time, with no Wellingtons, just hobnailed boots and leggings. Grandfather recalled walking home many a frosty winter's night with his clothes frozen on him. No wonder men were old at fifty or sixty and crippled with rheumatism. Grandfather was a handy rick-builder and once at threshing time he was building a load of straw on a farm waggon when the fore ladder broke. He fell on to the hard stone cobbles of the rickyard and fractured his skull. The ambulance which took him home unconscious was a muck-cart drawn by a carthorse from the bottom to the top of the village over the rough stone wheel ruts. He did no more work apart from working his allotment with the help of his donkey. But back to the Bradfields.

They were draining a field called Whitelands for Mr. Washbourne. The job was straightforward, they told George. They had plenty of fall for the drain to empty into the ditch by the barn. It was mid-winter and by half past four it would soon be knocking-off time. At just eighteen inches deep John struck the top of an earthenware pot with his graft and called Sep. The pot was full of golden coins in mint condition. Sep said, 'What bist a-gwain to do?' John said, 'Tell the gaffer a-course.' At Higford House Fred Washbourne was surprised to see the Bradfields back at the farm a bit early and so out of breath. 'Gaffer,' John spoke up, 'we a-found a pot of gold. Whatever be us to do?' Fred Washbourne thought quickly and told them not to touch it on any account or no good would come of it. 'Sep,' he said, 'you be wet through and you, John. Go home and change and have your tea. And here's two shillings to get something at the Plough and Harrow to warm you tonight.' 'Thank you, Gaffer,' said Sep. 'What about morning? Be us to carry on draining?' Fred Washbourne, telling them to carry on until the ground was finished, went in to his tea. John and Sep went to their cottage, promising Fred Washbourne that they would not tell a soul.

Coming from the Plough and Harrow that night Sep said to John, 'Thee look'st as red as a roost cock,' and John replied, 'Oi,

and thee bist as proud as Lucifer.' When they arrived at their
cottage John poured out two tots of metheglin as a nightcap
and they slept like two lords. At the drain the following morning Sep and John were a few minutes late. Making straight for
the spot where the pot of gold had been the night before they
found to their horror that it was gone.

From that day Fred Washbourne was always willing to give
them a load of farmyard muck for their allotment or lend them
two horses and a plough to plough their bit of stubble and a
horse and waggon to bring home their corn to stack in a little
round rick in the Plough and Harrow yard, along with all the
other allotment holders. There is no doubt that the best crop
that ever came off Whitelands was the pot of gold that Fred
Washbourne made good use of.

It was always said of the Bradfields that they were not afraid
of work, 'did their shot' and paid their whack'. Another of the
family, Job Bradfield, was a thatcher, a man and a half. To see
him raise his ladder, split his withies, draw his straw into over-
size boltings and carry them up on to the thatch of a cottage,
secure them with his shuppick and on the coldest of days start
peeling his clothes off to work until the sweat dropped off the
end of his nose was an inspiration. He kept a pig in a thatched
sty and grew it to about twenty score. He liked his bacon fat.
When he talked, he put in little phrases like, 'You understand
my meaning?', 'What I mean to say', 'Well, there it is', which
with one foot on the bottom rung of the ladder, his thumb stuck
under his broad leather belt with a brass buckle, gave him a sort
of dignified air. An interesting man, smart and upright, but not
a man to argue with.

One young fellow left our village to seek his fortune in the
iron foundries of the Black Country. Returning after a time he
visited the Plough and Harrow on a Saturday night. An argu-
ment developed between him and Job Bradfield. The returning
native described the villagers as a lot of swede gnawers knowing
nothing. Job invited him outside into the yard, and peeling off
showed him how much a swede gnawer knew of the noble art.
He knocked the 'townee', as he described him, 'ass over yud'.

But Job was a happy man at his work, singing as he went up and down the ladder, cutting and beating the thatch into shape. Some of his work still keeps out the snow and rain of winter and the gales of March and keeps the cottages cool when we do get any summer.

CHAPTER FOUR

THE DOCTOR AND THE ASHTON CLUB

DR. OVERTHROW lived in a three-storey early Victorian house in the middle of the village. Besides being a doctor, he was a district councillor, Guardian of the poor, J.P., Chairman of the School Board Parish Council; in fact, he had to a large extent taken the place of the Squire. As a young man he had been a clever surgeon. The older villagers swore by him, but when I knew him age and responsibility had made him forgetful and he remained Victorian in his methods. He always stressed to his patients how ill they had been and how lucky they were to survive.

But Dr. Overthrow was no ordinary doctor. His surgery window was close to the village street and he could be seen in there with his Edward VII beard, smoking cap, black coat with cloth-covered buttons (a frock coat, in fact), striped trousers and buttoned-up boots, mixing his medicines, pestle and mortar on the table. First one bottle would be fetched off the shelves and so many spots counted into his mixing bowl, followed by so many spots of something else. You could hear him counting on the road. Then, if one spot too many went into the mixture, he threw the lot down the drain to start all over again. Then came the shaking of the bottles, and when they were collected his advice was, 'Don't forget to give it a thundering good shaking before you take it.' That was a part of the treatment. The medicine was usually pleasant to take, tasting strongly of peppermint. Doctors, like the rest of us, get criticised, and the shepherd complained to me that Dr. Overthrow charged him three shillings for a bottle of medicine which was nothing in the world but a dose of salts.

The doctor enjoyed shooting and was an excellent shot. Just as it was nearing dusk one evening, someone told him that a deer was grazing on Gorse Hill. He took his gun and crept quietly under the big hedge next to the apple orchard and got within range of what appeared to be a deer. After firing both barrels he found out it was a cow crib. This tale got around and was added to a bit. A few days later, a rag, bone and rabbit-skin man called at the Plough and Harrow and enquired if any of the customers had any rabbit skins for sale. The landlord, being a gallus sort of man, said he knew the doctor had a very fine deer skin he would sell. The doctor soon tumbled to the identity of the practical joker and told him just what he thought of him.

He often carried his gun when visiting patients, as if to kill or cure. When there was a case of pneumonia in a neighbouring village and the doctor was going off shooting he would say, 'Let it stop until tonight. It will keep.' His logic was to see his patients late at night and at their worst. A neighbouring farmer ground him his linseed for poultices; the doctor was a great believer in poultices and pulled lots of his patients through pneumonia.

With Thomas Packer of Cheltenham in the 1870s, he was instrumental in starting a Sick and Dividend Club or Friendly Society, and he was the official doctor to the club. His surgery at the roadside was not well lighted and one night three youths went to be examined so that they could join the club. Other youths were out in the road looking through the uncurtained windows while the doctor went round them with a lighted candle after they had stripped off everything. The candle dropped wax on them, much to the amusement of the youths outside. I did say before that he was clever but very unorthodox, and he refused to pass one ex-serviceman whom he told, 'You have had rheumatic fever, my lad.' He was dead right.

But we are talking about a man who, in George V's reign, was still treating patients as in Victorian days, when hygiene was not a main feature of medical practice. A carter goes to him with a blister on his hand and the doctor cuts it with his scissors, not over a sink but over a polished table. 'Now you have spoilt my table,' says the doctor when the blister bursts. A neighbouring farmer called to see him one day and the doctor said, 'Come and have a drink, Sam,' taking down at random one of several blue bottles off the shelf, all marked 'poison'. Sam said, 'I am not having whisky out of that bottle. It's marked poison.' The doctor explained that he couldn't keep any whisky in the house unless he marked the bottle, 'poison'.

He drove on his rounds in a pony trap, more of a cob than a pony, a very fast animal indeed named Violet. Out late at night delivering babies, tending old people, he was a man for his time. He did his job knowing that lots of the poor would never pay him. He also had a sense of humour. David, his gardener, was planting his potatoes and the doctor said, 'Are you sure you are putting those potatoes far enough apart?' 'Quite sure, doctor. Some I be planting in your garden and some in mine.'

When the doctor had a meeting at Evesham, Violet would be waiting, ready to take him to the station. But the doctor rarely left before the train was coming out of the next station two miles away. Then, with his son driving, he came at full gallop past our house, his son shouting, 'Violet, Violet, you wasted life. Do you think I stole you?' Sometimes the train would be leaving the station and wait for him along by the sidings.

As I have mentioned, he was often out very late at night when babies were being born. On one occasion a local brick-layer's wife was expecting her first child. Latish at night it seemed that the baby would not be long and when the midwife, Betsy Bradfield was called, she told the father to fetch Dr. Overthrow. The doctor had gone to bed. Syd Burge shouted up to his window, 'Doctor, it's the missus. She's having her baby.' The doctor said 'Get back to bed, man, you are all the same with the first, impatient. She is not due for a fortnight. It's indigestion. Give her some peppermint in hot water and get back to bed. When the apple's ripe it will fall.' Syd went home. Betsy said, 'Is he coming?' Syd said, 'No, it isn't due.' Betsy said, 'Tell him I said come quickly.' Syd went again for the doctor who said, 'If Betsy says so, it's time for me to come.' A baby girl was born at three a.m. The doctor went back to bed and slept until mid-day missing, as he said, meeting King

Edward VII on an official visit to Gloucester.

When council elections were near the doctor, when canvassing, reminded his patients that their bills were due. Very few paid and he was never defeated.

The Sick and Dividend Club met on Whit Wednesday. Here is an extract from a parish magazine: 'The annual gathering of the Ashton-under-Hill Friendly Society took place on Wednesday. The members, led by the Band and Banner, attended service at Church, then paraded the village and afterwards sat down to a sumptuous dinner in a marquee in the grounds of the Plough and Harrow. Dr. Overthrow creditably discharged the duties in the chair. The usual toasts were given and responded to heartily by the visitors and officers, including the Vicar and Curate who took part. The balance sheet showed the Society to be in a strong financial position. Amusement was duly provided for young and old and a very good day was marked by goodwill and sobriety.'

The amusements referred to were Scarrots Ginny Horses, which revolved by means of a man turning a wheel, and swinging boats, always a great attraction for the not quite grown-ups. My cousin, Nellie Breeze, from London came down to Grandfather's for club day and, of course, living at Tooting, had lost the local accent. Young Ern Adamson took her up in the swinging boats. He had been sweethearting her the evening before, and showing concern about whether she was being taken up too high, asked her politely, 'Bist a feeling sick?' and Nellie in a very affected voice replied, 'Jest ay trifle.'

'Sobriety,' reported the parish magazine. This must have been an exceptional year, for usually all the farmers and people of means put jugs of ale, cider, metheglin, rhubarb and parsnip wine for anyone to take. Sometimes the band were overcome by the generosity of the Ashton folk. Alderton had no difficulty in getting their bandsmen home but Corse Lawn, who could play Colonel Bogey with the next, had a drop too much one club day. Their band started late for home and decided to cross the Avon at Twyning Fleet. They were unstable in the ferry boat which tipped over just before they reached the opposite bank and they lost most of their instruments in the river.

A lot of supporters of the club came from Cheltenham in what were known as the Grand Carriages, pulled by two lovely sleek horses abreast. As the carriages were loading up ready to start the return journey home eleven miles to Cheltenham, the horses, bedecked with blue Tory ribbons, would be scauting with their forefeet, impatient to leave the Plough and Harrow, in fact raring to go. Then down the village street they came, as old Charlie Bradfield told me, hell for leather. What a break from the monotony of work was Ashton Club! Apart from official organisation these clubs and wakes had a following of cheap-jacks, medicine men and boxing booths. At Club Days many a young man met the girl he would eventually walk down the aisle of St. Barbara's Church. Uncouth and uncultured as they were, they are the ancestors of some of us living here today.

CHAPTER FIVE

WALT

WALT, OUR CARTER, had eight working horses, two nags and an old pony to look after when I first knew him. He lived up at Paris, a little hamlet up on the hill, and he carried his coal, paraffin, bread, in fact everything, up through the young orchard of Bramley apples, then on across Boss Close, up the narrow path to his cottage. I thought years since that I never saw Walt go home from work without having something to carry. 'I s'pose I shall 'a to hump this half-hundredweight of coal up tonight,' he remarked as he got his back under the bag that Bill Drinkwater had left for him on the wall by the thatched cart house. So with either a Woodbine or a pipe of Red Bell and his back bent he made for home, a half mile tramp saying, 'Shan't be sorry to have a cup of tay.'

Walt fetched his water from the spring, had no modern sanitation, grew his own potatoes, fetched his horses in at five o'clock in the morning and worked until dark, haymaking and harvest.

When I left school I had already worked with Walt, riding the foremost horse on the binder and leading old Flower, horse-hoeing brussel sprouts—ding dong all day. There was just an occasional stop to light Walt's pipe. Then with a click of his tongue he would shout, 'Go ahead! You can't do too much for a good master.' We were away, starting another bout, or there and back down the rows of sprouts. 'Push her yud off a bit, Fred,' he blurted out at times when I was perhaps thinking of other things than sprout skimming and was letting Flower get too near to the left. Then, 'Pull her yud towards ya a bit. The ground's a bit sideland.' He was on the dot at lunch-time and by half past five I don't know whether his legs ached. Mine did.

The month I left school in 1931 our ploughboy got himself a job as under-gardener at a big house in the next village so I was sent as Walt's ploughboy. I thought that everything there was to learn about horses I knew, but was soon disillusioned when we went to plough with four horses. The ground had been ploughed in the autumn and we were ploughing it back in March. A cold biting wind blew. Walt said it was a 'skinny wind from Russia'. Our team was Turpin foremost, Boxer and Bonnie Body and Lash Horse in the middle of the team and old Captain Filler drawing up the rear. First of all, the walking was bad. We were ploughing back and walking on the old furrows. I wore out a ten-shilling pair of boots in the first week. Walt said the ground mooted or muffled, which meant it didn't slip cleanly off the sheel board of the plough and he had to clean the clay off with the plough paddle kept for this purpose in a little ledge in the throat of the plough.

The team pulled evenly until we came to the 'addledum' or headland, when with whip in hand and walking backwards I led Turpin first up to the hedge, turned, 'come agun' or to the left and timed it so that each horse did his whack and pulled the plough as far as it could before following Turpin at right angles to the furrow along the headland. If I had kept Turpin's traces tight the next horse would have followed without going to the end. The first three horses did as they were supposed to and it was left for Captain, the filler, to pull the plough himself the last few yards. Walt started shouting, 'Aw, come 'ee back,' as Captain ran off into the ploughed ground and the plough ran easy but made a nasty crook in the furrow. I hadn't kept the traces of the middle horses tight enough by shouting 'Come on, Boxer. Yup, Flower,' and cracking the whip. If this happened many times Walt said, 'We 'a got a furrow crookeder than a dog's hind leg,' and we had to take some pikes or short turns to right matters. This was done by turning the team and ploughing the last few yards again. It's enough to make me run my country and if I was single I'd 'list for a soldier,' Walt said. Ploughing never went just right for Walt. He liked to see the clay soil come up shining like rashers of bacon, an unbroken furrow from one end of the ground to the other.

Captain was experienced; I was green and if I cracked the whip Turpin would take me through the hedge. He was a powerful gelding and it was not unusual for him to break the traces. All these horses were related in some way; Boxer and Turpin were brothers, both by Bishampton Harold out of Bonnie, who went lame and did jobs pottering round the farm. After a time we got a better understanding, Walt, me, Flower, Boxer, Captain and Turpin. Dad and Mr. Carter were pleased with the way I was shaping. In those days I went to work in a pair of Bedford cord breeches, puttees and hobnailed boots; I had a Derby tweed jacket with a poacher's pocket and I felt no end of a fellow. Dad said, 'I reckon Fred ought to go in for a parson as he doesn't care whether the cow calves or the bull breaks his neck.' But I almost decided farming wasn't for me. The work was long and tedious and there always was in winter a great weight of clay soil sticking to my boots. I was a smallish lad; Walt told me to go to the bull-pen and stand in the bull muck and I should shoot up like a poplar tree.

Now Walt had a wonderful assortment of boots in the harness room near the stable. Some had pieces cut out of them to ease his corns and bunions. At sheep-shearing time he fetched out of the Cross barn a fleece of wool off old Shepherd Corbisley. He packed his boots with wool and toe rags. No doubt his feet were painful and after ploughing some nights, as we sat on the bench in the harness room while the horses munched at their chopped bait of chaff, mangolds and oat flour, old Walt would say, 'My fit be that sore, they be just like liver. Ast got ere a Woodbine? I ant got one, nor a wift a 'bacca.' I kept a few for him (and had an occasional one myself) and fetched his Red Bell tobacco, threepence halfpenny for half an ounce, from the village shop.

Walt was usually last to fetch his money from our court window on a Friday night and Dad would be seated at the big table in the hall as the envelopes disappeared one by one (I mean the pay packets). Dad would say to me, 'I wonder what Walt will have to say tonight.' I have heard something like this. 'Well,

Master, ant that ploughing gone bad! I've never had a job like that afore. Stick, moot, clog, no slip to it,' and rubbing his bare arms, he added 'and ant that gen my arms summat. Another day or two like this un and I'll be on the box.' Dad would say, 'When do you think you will finish the job, Walt?' 'Finish it! It won't be next wick. And what about some corn for my 'osses? Master Carter won't let me start the clover rick and they'll soon be as thin as hurdles.' Dad would reply, 'I'll see Mr. Carter starts a cut on the clover rick but be careful. Mind, it's a long while till May Day.'

Saturday mornings I usually took one or two horses to the blacksmith's to have them reshod. That was a day out. I rode. I went full of instructions from Walt. 'Bring me some cart nails, some horse nail stubbs and shut links.' The cart nails were to act as wedges to stop plough-wheel stems from slipping in their iron collars or the same for skim or scuffle wheels. Horse-nail stubbs were handy to drive in between the link of the trace and the wooden spreader to save spreader pegs. Shut links were like split rings used as a temporary repair for long gears or trace harness. The shut link was linked to the two broken ends of the trace and closed up to form an extra link. If you long to hear of the simple tackle, this is it, all from the village blacksmith who had no welding apparatus but shut two white-hot pieces of iron together to form his weld, hammering them on the anvil until they became one piece.

When we had ploughed back the Thurness twenty-one acres at the rate of three-quarters of an acre a day the partners, Mr. Carter and Dad, decided that a scuffling both ways with a nine-tined Larkworthy scuffle would kill the squitch (couch grass) and get the ground in good order. Walt and I put four horses, two abreast, on this heavy implement which brought up big 'clats' of clay for the wind and sun to 'lax'. We had Turpin and Boxer on the front coupled together by a coupling stick. I had to lead these and Captain and Old Dick with his big knee behind. Walt drove these with a pair of cord reins known as G.O. lines.

Now Boxer and Turpin, although they were brothers got by

the famous Bishampton Harold, were about as much alike as chalk and cheese. Turpin was always raring to go. One word and he lurched forward; a crack of the whip and he would pull me almost under his feet. Boxer was Walt's pet and he knew it; he lagged behind Turpin about a yard and made the foremost pair of our team look untidy. I touched him up a bit with the whip sometimes, but Walt said, 'Don't thee get a waling that hoss. He's a doing his shot.' Old Dick was a biter. He would have gone as a war horse in 1914 but for his big knee. He matched Captain who had a ridged back like a camel, as I found to my discomfort riding him down the hill from haymaking. His backbons was knobbly and the action of this was like that of a crosscut saw.

We cleaned the Thurness that Spring, Walt finishing the job by giving it the once-over with the duckfoot drags, a heavy harrow with feet like ducks. He didn't need me for this as he drove three horses abreast.

Walt was a wit and at the last Harvest Supper, a joint affair to be held in our village, Fred Pickford asked if anybody wanted any more food. The men having had just about as much as they could manage, Walt said, 'Yes, gaffer. I do.' A hush went over the gathering and Walt waited a few seconds before he added, 'Tomorrow night.' He could sing a song himself and I loved to hear him at the village concerts sing,

> 'I love the green fields
> And I love the sunshine,
> The robin with pretty red breast;
> I love pussy cat
> Fast asleep on the mat,
> But I love my dear mother the best.'

As a carter, he treated his ploughboys fairly although he had a hard upbringing himself. As a boy he worked for a farmer who took pigs to a distant village in a cider barrel because there was an outbreak of swine fever in the village and a 'standstill' order. The farmer treated him hard, made him sleep in an attic and didn't allow him a candle for fear of fire. Breakfast was of cider sop, or bread soaked in cider, and the carter he worked under thought nothing of giving him a stroke or two with the horse whip. I like to picture Walt mowing. The day before, Walt sorted out his G.O. gears (light trace harness). We had two sets of leather-covered wire traces, ex-artillery from the 1914 war. These were ideal for working two horses double-fixed into what were known as body hames. Body hames were for trace harness but could be used for fillers tack by using false togs (short chains like miniature traces about fifteen inches long). All Walt needed to keep the traces up was a back band of leather, the traces threading through two loops at either end of this. The horses hitched on to 'supple' trees at the back end of the pole and two large leather straps at the front end of the pole were fastened through the bottom of each horse's collar taking some weight on the crest of the horse's neck. Walt was a little man and his weight was not enough when he sat on the mowing machine seat to balance the weigh. This meant extra weight on what he called the horse's 'cresses'. Despite the fact that he suspended a fifty-six pound weight from the back of his seat, their cresses still got sore with this weight. In fact the machine was badly balanced. Walt rubbed alum on the sores to harden the skin and fortunately we had plenty of horses and he was able to change about. As soon as we approached Pleasant, a spirited mare, with her harness she would lay back her ears and start to kick. Dad and Mr. Carter got another reconditioned machine. (They never bought anything new as long as I can remember except a hay-loader.) Walt was happy. He started on the First Ham, then the Far Ham, and he told me, 'That fresh mower gus clinking. But, my goy, unt it a job, a' them wet ant humps. They clogs the knife up every feow yards down by Carrants Brook.' When you saw Walt with his favourite pair, the brothers Boxer and Turpin, they made a fine sight. Turpin was a liver chestnut with massive shoulders. We hadn't got a collar big enough for him and Albert Grimmit, the Beckford saddler, came up and measured him for a new one. Boxer, a true chestnut about sixteen hands compared with Turpin's seven-

teen, was Walt's spoilt child. He thought that little bit extra of
Boxer. When the bree flies and 'old maids' (horse flies) were
'laying holt', as Walt put it, these horses, swishing their tails,
took Walt round the field at almost a jog trot. The view from
the front was a mass of elderberry blossom laced around the
horses' 'mullins' to keep some of the flies from around their
eyes, ears and noses, but every time Walt got off his machine to
oil up he smacked the horses' briskets with his hands, killing
these bloodsuckers and the bree flies which laid their eggs on the
feather part of the leg above the hocks. Sometimes the 'old
maids' sampled the blood from Walt's arms which were bare to
his elbows. 'Tell yer father that fust ground I cut wants moving
with the swath turner. We'm a gwain to get a rattle afore long.'
I knew he meant thunder and as he spoke a whirly wind took
some of the partly-made hay up into the air almost out of sight.
He started his mowing early, often at first light; and when the
mid-day sun was pouring down on man and beast the horses
were rested in the shade while Walt went hay pitching; then he
went on mowing in the cool of the evening. His frail at haymaking, which he hung on the horse's hames as he left the stable
and then put in some shady spot for bait time, was both a food
basket and a tool bag. Besides his food and drink, he carried an
oil can, a screw spanner, shut links, mowing-machine blade sections, a file, a punch and a hammer. He carried out all small
repairs in the field, but if there was anything more serious he'd
say, 'Fred, gu down to Segebrra and fetch young Tom Harris.'
Tom was the blacksmith and came on a motor-bike and box side-
car. Although Walt called him young, he must have been knock-
ing on for seventy, but you see Walt knew his father and Tom
would always be young Tom.

I like to think of Walt also in the winter time just before old
Shepherd Corbisley's ewes started lambing. The shepherd had to
be waited on and Walt and his ' 'osses' and the narrow-wheeled
waggon were the means of transporting the shepherds' tackle
about. One morning in late January Mr. Carter met me outside
the gear house of the stable and said, 'Fred, I want you to give
Walt a hand today. The shepherd wants his troughs, wire and

hurdles moved up to the Grest Hill and he'll need four horses
on the waggon.' I thought this would be, as Walt would say,
'like a job in the town'.

Captain was chosen to go in the waggon shafts as filler. The
cart saddle fitted snugly on his ridged back, in front of his
hump like a camel's. This made no difference to his great
strength but kept him, in company with Dick, from going as a
war horse in 1914. After the horses had been watered at the pool
I helped Walt shut Captain in between the waggon shafts. We
lifted the shafts to the right height after Walt had backed Captain into position. 'Throw us the ridge chain over steady and
don't hit me on top of the yud with it.' I fastened the togs but
left Walt to do up the breechings, for we had some steep hills to
come down and they had to be made safe. The waggon had been
partly loaded the day before, supervised by the shepherd, but we
had to call at the hurdle makers on the way up the hill to pick
up some new hurdles he had made out of a load of withy poles
we had taken him some weeks before. Walt sent me back to the
stable to fetch his straw frail and the shut links which were
hung up in the gear house on a nail. 'We had better take 'um.
Old Turpin on the front 'ull bound to snatch going up the
gully,' he said. Walt was meanwhile up on the clover rick cutting a kerf of hay to put on the back of the waggon for the
horses' dinner.

'Now, Fred, take a rick peg and yer's my shut knife. Flatten
the one end of the peg, get some cart grease out of the cart
house and with the rick peg put plenty of grease on the guides
of the waggon. Put some on the axles. They be got dry and
don't they ever holler! We don't want everybody to yur us a-
coming.'

Walt hung his frail containing his bait and dinner on Captain's hames. Peeping out of the top was a quart bottle of tea
with the legend 'Vat 69' on the label. The usual things were also
in there, but most important today were the shut links. I put my
haversack on Turpin's harness. Walt threw a faggot of wood
out of the pile in the rickyard for making a fire at dinner-time.
This he placed on the tailboard of the waggon on top of the kerf

of hay. I put my 410 gun carefully in one of the sheep troughs. There might be the chance of a rabbit. 'Hook Turpin in front of Boxer and old Flower and we'll get off. The shepherd'll be waiting.'

We started on our way. I had a leading rein on Turpin and walked by the side of Boxer, with a brand-new whip from Albert Grimmits hanging round my neck. Walt, walking by the side of the filler, Captain, watched the trace horses take the strain with an experienced eye to see if they were all pulling level. 'We don't want none on 'um to get sore shoulders,' he said. 'Woa, take Boxer's traces up one more link on this side. That makes three spare links hanging on each side. That's better. We don't want to get him pinched' (a term used for sore shoulders). When we arrived at Lofty Summer's, the ladder and hurdle makers, we loaded the new hurdles on top of the waggon. How clean and white they looked as we carried them from under his walnut tree and roped our load again! We moved off up the eastern slopes of Bredon Hill. The first steep part was at Paris and I held Turpin's leading rein tighter as he broke into a jog-trot round the bend by Modeleys. They slowed down a bit halfway up this bank and Walt said, 'Just touch old Boxer up a bit with that whip.' I cracked it and Boxer just nodded his head up and down as much to say, you dare touch me, but Turpin lounged forward and his traces tightened with such a snatch I thought they would break and we would be needing the shut links.

Now there had been a frost and it was going fast as the sun got up and we approached Paris barn. There were two ways we could go round the barn; to the right was not as steep, but the grass was slippery as the frost was going. Walt said, 'Keep 'um to the left. Wau, come 'ee back,' and we went up the wheel ruts to the left. Next came a level stretch on Quar Hill. 'Whoa,' said Walt. 'Let 'um have a blow and I'll have a Woodbine. Hast got any matches?' I'd got some matches. Off again and the next half mile up the Leasow was really steep. Walt told me, 'Keep 'um going, mind, up the middle gateway. We don't want to get stuck there and make them two help on the front. Old Flower's all of a lather and you knows her's a bit broken winded.'

We charged up through the gateway. Turpin led the way, almost on his knees and ankle deep in mud. The steam was rising from his broad shoulders and a trace of lathering foam was now showing under his crupper and more under his belly-band.

After we had gone through the deep gully on Spring Hill, the waggon rocking and rolling over the loose stones, we came to nearly a mile of almost flat going, and after the horses had been given another blow to get their wind, Walt said, 'We'll ride and rest my legs.' He gave me a leg-up on to Turpin's back and I dug my heels into the traces. He then put a pair of G.O. lines on Captain and climbed on the front of the waggon.

Over the brow of the next little hill just on the skyline a figure was moving towards us. It was Shepherd Corbisley. 'Morning Shepherd. It's cold up yer,' Walt said. 'My Goy, it ketches holt of my y'ers.' 'It was fust thing,' the shepherd replied. 'Smartish frost and we shall get a duck's frost tonight. This is the third white un we've had.'

The shepherd then put one foot on one of the spokes of the waggon wheel and looked at his new hurdles. As he chewed his twist and spat I could see he wasn't too happy. 'I told old Lofty,' he started off, 'not to make the fit of them hurdles so long, but he took no notice. How can I get 'um in the ground up yer among all this stone?' We moved off silently until we arrived at the sprout field where the men were finishing the early sprouts. Shepherd Corbisley was going to put up the wire and hurdles and hitch off the stems a pen at a time with his tegs (last year's lambs). Walt and I had to bring a load of sprouts down the hill on the waggon at night.

Walt said as he climbed off the waggon, 'Whur dust want the troughs and hurdles?' The shepherd told us to drop them off handy as he didn't want to carry them too far. We unloaded and it was bait time.

We sat down on a couple of empty sacks under a dry stone wall. We were in the burrow for half an hour. The larks were twittering as they ascended into an almost cloudless sky. The linnets were singing their sweet little song in the few stunted hawthorn bushes. But it was one of Tustin's weather breeders. Walt said, 'Look yonder, Shepherd, towards the tower. I reckon you be gwain to be right. The crows be at breaknecks.' A whole flock of them were circling at great height and diving down like dive bombers. 'Oi,' the shepherd said, 'they be a cider-making up thur.' All the time they were cawing furiously, a sign of rain. 'No wonder my fit aches,' Walt said. As we drank our luke-warm tea I had rosemary-flavoured bread and lard and Walt ate his bread (the top of a cottage loaf) and cheese with a bone-handled shut knife cutting it in thumb pieces. The shepherd had some beetroot wine with his bait and gave some to Walt and between them they put the world right. The shepherd was still talking about Lofty and the too-long feet he had made for the hurdles. Then Walt said, 'Hast got 'ere a wift a 'bacca?' and they lit their short clay pipes. We worked with the shepherd after lunch and as he told us tales out of *Tit-Bits* the time went fast. We rolled the wire out and he put the stakes in.

'Did I ever tell ya,' he said, 'about that bloke at Chadbury who axed me to shear his sow pig?' 'No,' I said. 'Well, I told him I'd do it on condition he rolled the fleece up after but he 'udn't take on that un.'

Our branch railway line was out of sight behind Grafton firs so we couldn't tell the time by the trains. We could see the trains on what Walt called the New Line, Laverton way, but as I watched them disappear into a tunnel towards Cheltenham I didn't know what times they ran.

The shepherd said, 'It's about dinner-time,' and I made a fire with the faggot of wood in the old stone quarry. Walt said, 'It'd be borougher there.' The horses were given the kerf of clover. We pointed two rick pegs and toasted our bacon over the fire using the pegs as toasting forks. Our tea was now stone cold but the bread and bacon went down well and in the burrow we were again out of the cold wind. We put a few of last year's sprout stems on the fire just to make a 'blizzy', had a good warm and started loading our waggon with sprouts. The bags weighed forty pounds each of sprouts. At about a quarter to five Walt said to the sprout pickers, 'Have you chaps a'mus done for today cos I'm a-going down with my load now? We shall have it dark and I have got to go to the station with this lot.' The load being on the waggon, we started for home. As I said before, the first half-mile was fairly flat and the horses stepped along briskly and the old waggon creaked and groaned as it jolted over the stones in the rough cart track. At every little decline we came to, Captain sat well back in the breeching and kept the load back steadily. This is why Captain was filler. He was a tower of strength and acted almost like an anchor, holding back a terrific weight when it was necessary. We came to the gully on Spring hill, where the road winds its way down an escarpment and is bounded on either side by a steep bank of stone and earth. This fills level with snow in a hard winter. Walt shouted 'Whoa!' but the horses were loath to stop. Their heads were towards home and it was nearly their tea-time. Walt then locked the nearside hind wheel with the huge chain provided for the purpose and put the skid pan in position under the wheel. This was to prevent the iron waggon tyre from being worn out of shape on the rough stones. At this point he also locked the offside wheel with the chain provided. Then, with Captain sitting well back in the breeching, we moved slowly down the very steep part of the hill.

How the locked wheels screeched as they slid over the Cotswold stone wheel ruts! And as dusk fell and the first evening star appeared over Cleeve Hill the cock pheasant could be heard going up to roost in Ashton Wood, 'cock up, cock up'. Sparks were now flying from the hind wheels when a harder flint was crushed by the weight of the waggon loaded with sprouts. Sparks were also coming from the shoes of the four horses as they clip-clopped along the middle of the track.

Just as Walt said to me, 'I shall be late coming back from the station tonight,' we went through a stream of water running from a spring coming out of the side of the hill. The iron tyres on the rear of the waggon were hot by now and clouds of steam rose from behind as we passed the stream.

As long as the waggon followed the wheel ruts, it ran straight with both wheels locked; but we came out of the ruts at this point and the breech of the waggon, as Walt said, slewed round at an angle on the slippery turf. Walt stopped the horses. 'Make old Captain hold back,' he said, and he unlocked the offside wheel. Captain now had to do a little more holding back of the load with the breeching. We passed the Sheep Wash Pool, Shaw Green, and then were in Cottons Lane.

The first tarmac had just been laid in the village street and the now nearly red-hot skid pan was sizzling, the tar introducing yet another smell to blend with the smell of the sprouts, the horses and Walt's Woodbine. We left a skid mark six inches wide as we went. The oil lamps were burning in the cottage windows and Walt said, 'I shall soon be up the wooden hill when I've had my tay and I shan't need no rocking to get to sleep neither.'

I left Walt at the Village cross having unhooked the three trace horses. Then I took them down to the stable, gave them some water, lit the lantern in the gear house, and gave them the chopped bait that Walt had prepared early that morning. Walt took the waggon-load of sprouts to the station with Captain and loaded them in a truck for Nottingham.

There will never be another Walt. I still meet him now, one of the very last of the old school who have always lived close to the soil. He is bent and a bit deaf but still keeps a lively interest in crops and livestock. 'What sort a' luck be ya having with yer lambing' is a question he asks me every Spring and I shall be sorry when he's no longer with us and no longer able to care. When he can, he does his garden, plants his potatoes, worries about them until they are dug and picks his one pear tree. What a good thing he still interests himself with living and growing things! 'Life's allus bin the same, ever since Adam was a byoy' was his favourite saying.

CHAPTER SIX

WILLUM ARCHER AND POLLY OLIVER

WILLUM OR FARLEY ARCHER was a cousin of Grandfather's and lived in a cottage adjoining the main Cheltenham road with his housekeeper, Polly Oliver. I knew him in the 1920s but he was so primitive that he might have been Thomas Hardy's Granfer Cantle in *The Return of the Native*. The cottage was not only occupied by Farley and Polly but by his hens and his cats. The hens roosted around his fireside, nested in his easy chairs, and Neddy, his donkey, was stabled in the little slated barn up the garden. Farley was quite a regular visitor to our house and as I picture him now in his working clothes—I never saw him dressed up—I wonder whether he ever existed (but he did). His billycock hat was tied on to his head with a piece of binder twine, probably to prevent it falling off when he was working his land, about four acres in Carrants Field. His other clothes were black gone green with age and his coat had cloth-covered buttons. This was a typical funeral outfit of years back. When he took off his coat he had underneath what was known as a ganzy or cardigan, a mixture of black and white with buff-coloured bone buttons. He was a stocky, upright man, like many of our family, about five feet eight inches tall. Polly Oliver was deaf and dumb and short and stout; she wore a brown hurden apron around her ample waist, carried a writing slate and slate pencil wherever she went, took snuff and backed horses.

As Farley had only a donkey on his four acres he had a lot of hard work to do, but we ploughed his land with our team of horses. Walt, our carter, when he was having his bait sitting in the borough of Farley's hedge after ploughing from just after seven o'clock in the morning, was surprised to see Farley cross the main road from his cottage to his allotment carrying a large jug. This was filled with cocoa with lumps of toast floating

about on top. 'Yer thee bist, Walt, get that into tha. It will keep
the cold out,' Farley said. As soon as Farley's back was turned
Walt poured the mixture over the plough wheels. I don't think
anyone could have relished any food or drink which came from
that cottage. Enfield Cottage, which it is called, reeked of fer-
mentation. Hogshead barrels sawn in half to make tubs stood in
a little semicircle round the door out in the yard. These contained wines in various stages, parsnip, rhubarb, plum, jerkum,
all bubbling and fizzing. Fowls perched even in the rims of these
tubs, the contents eventually to be poured into his barrels in the
barn. Farley often was in a muddled state mixing his drinks. He
kept a couple of hives of bees under the damson trees up the
garden and after he had extracted the honey from the combs he
boiled the honeycombs in water in his copper furnace and next
morning skimmed the beeswax off the top of the liquid and put
the liquid in a little four-and-a-half-gallon cask to become
metheglin, a kind of mead.

Sometimes Polly Oliver came to our door with these words
written on her slate to my father: 'Tom, 'ull you lend me a
couple of men? We be gwain a-threshing tomorrow.' Dad
usually obliged. Farley's threshing was a bit of a joke. He got
the threshing tackle there from a neighbouring village and
Bertie Johnson had got steam up by seven o'clock in the morning waiting to start. 'Where be the men, Farley?' said Bertie.
'Don't know,' he replied. Bertie said, 'Hasn't axed anybody to
come and help tha, Farley?' 'No, that I ant,' said Farley. 'They
shouldn't need no axing. I'd a thought anybody uda come and
helped me to thresh.' Another time he arranged to start threshing at eight o'clock to give him time to get the thatch off his
rick. The engine-driver was there getting up steam at seven and
Farley was busy stripping the thatch off his little round rick of
wheat when Polly Oliver arrived ready to start work. Farley saw
her coming from his vantage place on the rick and shouted at
her 'Bless the 'ooman, if thee hadst a-come an hour agu thee
udst a-bin plenty sun enough.' His labels on his market produce
caused many a laugh and he sent some runner beans into
Evesham market one August labelled as four pots of Painted

Ladies (the variety).

People will tell you they have never seen a dead donkey. Well, Farley's donkey died and he was soon at our house. He said he was all behind with his work already and he used this donkey with Polly leading it on his breast plough to clean his stubble and harrow up the rubbish to burn. 'Tom,' he said to Dad. 'Ut thee send Walt down to skim a bit of ground ready for my runner byeans?' Walt went down with two horses, Prince and Bonnie, and the big two-wheeled skim and raised enough mould to plant the beans. Farley was busy digging a hole to bury old Neddy. 'He ant finished work for me yet,' Farley said, 'and I beunt a-gwain to put him in very dip.' Walt was thunderstruck at what he witnessed. Farley buried the donkey with his four legs sticking up in the air. Walt said, 'Why doesn't put him in dipper than that?' 'Ah,' said Farley, 'I be gwain to grow some runner byeans up his four legs this year.'

Farley could lay a hedge, dig a ditch, unstop a drain, but he was no builder. Two things he needed: one was a shed on his ground to shelter and keep his tools in; another was a privy up the garden. He built the shed first and was priding himself on his workmanship when he needed the wheelbarrow to fetch his onions from the bottom of his ground. When he went to get the barrow it would not come through the door, the doorway being too narrow, and he had to knock the side of his shed out to get his wheelbarrow. He then built his privy or earth closet and still made the doorway so narrow that he had no room to turn round and had to reverse into it.

I suppose Farley and Polly had a fair living in their grubby way. They always kept a good pig and had a swill tub by the back door where all the cabbage water leftovers and potato peelings went to add another unwholesome smell to the surrounds of Enfield Cottage. They neither of them, Farley nor Polly, died of typhoid nor food poisoning, and as far as I knew never had the doctor. Polly backed horses, as I said earlier, and Farley studied the stars and both of them faded away with old age.

CHAPTER SEVEN

PONTO

PONTO, I GATHER, was born of respectable parents at Honey-suckle Cottage, his father being an insurance agent. As a lad he became a strapper or under-groom at some race-horse stables the other side of the hill at Woolas Hall. Being crossed in love for Sue Hill was his undoing, for from then on he became an oddity.

He was a little man and he worked when he felt like it, doing jobs on the farms normally done by boys; leading horses at mangold and muck-cart, driving horses at plough, bird mind-ing, running errands. Being simple-minded he was made a source of amusement by people who should have known better. It's a strange fact that some of these people when they got older became little better than Ponto.

As a boy I was sometimes afraid when Ponto, then an old man, would be running a group of lads who had been teasing him. When he worked for us he slept in a farm waggon in the cart shed, lived in the daytime in the little gear- or harness-room attached to our stable. Here he had his meals. We cooked his Sunday dinner and he cooked his usual mid-day meal, fried over a fire in the field. At tea-time he came to our window for a jug of tea, and he had several calling places in the village where they took pity on him and in this way he got by. He had a good appetite and when rationing was introduced during the 1914–18 war Ponto was in real trouble. He drew his week's rations from the village shop and got through the lot in about two days. When he went for more and was told he had had his allowance for that week, he kicked the door saying he 'allus had what he wanted when Mrs. Hook kept the shop'. Dad then took over his ration card and doled his rationed food out day by day. He used to come to our back window in the summer-time and say to

Mother, 'I be thirsty, mam, very thirsty.' Mother gave him some jelly one day and he came back and said, 'Have you got any more a that shaky stuff to spare, mam?'

He had a round rosy face and about two teeth and an engaging grin; people living in houses with their own fireside couldn't help feeling sorry for him. But if anything went wrong in the village, the youths and young men out of devilment always said it was Ponto's fault and, of course, he took it seriously. One day someone's pig choked itself with a swede or something. 'Who choked the pig?' the lads said. 'Ponto choke pig.' To calls of 'Ponto choke pig', he chased the mob down the village street and I was called indoors as his language was not considered fit for me to hear. Mrs. Stanton's donkey fell into the little quarry on Quar Hill and broke its back. The lads said Ponto had pushed it over. 'Who pushed Mrs. Stanton's donkey in the quarry?' 'Ponto,' the others would answer, and with a stick or anything he could lay his hands on he came charging after the group of youths, then to our house to tell Dad all about it. 'As you knows, Master Archer, I udn't harm no donkey.' Dad would reassure him and things would quieten down for a bit.

Ponto had a constant fear of the Russians. 'The Rueshans' he called them and he blamed them for things that happened that he could not explain. He left his matches on top of a stone wall on Bredon Hill in a field at the back of Grafton Firs. The sun shining through his bottle on to the matches ignited them. Ponto was leading a horse called Prince for Walt, our carter, but he refused to do any more work that day saying, 'It's them Rueshans.'

Our village stationmaster got involved in this teasing of Ponto. He sent the porter to Ponto's lodgings with a telegram to say his brother was despatching a hamper of food and clothing to our station. Dad was told it included hams or bacon, cheeses, shirts and trousers, and poor old Ponto trudged the half-mile there and back many times to meet one passenger train after another, and of course nothing ever arrived. I thought the stationmaster a bit mean when he told Ponto the goods had been put off at Ashchurch by mistake and Ponto walked six miles each way to Ashchurch just on a wild goose chase. I have written before about home-made fun and humour. Practical jokes of this kind are not funny but they had their place in the rough and tumble of village life as it was then.

As a very small boy I only teased Ponto once. It was a Sunday morning and the usual crop of dogstools (toadstools) was growing on the steaming heap of horse manure outside our stable. I pulled up some of these and took them to Ponto, asking if he fancied mushrooms for breakfast. He chased me, caught me outside our back gate and gave me a swipe with his stick. I didn't tell Dad or else I might have been in further trouble.

Ponto didn't always sleep in our waggon but moved from place to place. One of his haunts was Syd Burge's pigsty. Now, Syd had warned Ponto to keep out; the place had a thatched roof and he was afraid of Ponto starting a fire. Ponto persisted in staying there and kept all his junk and spare clothes in the sty. One Saturday afternoon, after the Plough and Harrow had turned out Ponto, a regular customer for his cider, Syd got a few pals together and told Ponto he was going to sell these belongings to pay for his rent. The auction started outside Syd's sty. 'How much for this pair of shoes?' It was knocked down to one of Syd's friends for half a crown. Ponto went frantic. 'They be selling me up carpet bag and all.' The carpet bag had another story attached to it. The police questioned Ponto once where he had got it from and had this reply, 'Ah, you thinks I pinched it, don't ya, but I had it given me for cleaning out Master Blackwell's closet.'

April Fool's Day was another opportunity to pull Ponto's leg. A farmer would put some stones in a sack and send Ponto with it to the next farm. This farmer would say a mistake had been made and send him in turn to the next. They would give him a drink of cider—and one wonders who was the bigger fool, the farmers or Ponto. There are so many stories about Ponto. I well remember how he'd come round carol-singing at Christmas. 'Wild shapeherds Watch,' he sang.

A near tragedy happened one summer's night. The lads from the Plough and Harrow told Ponto the devil had been seen in the churchyard and that he was in some ivy at the back of an old gravestone. Ponto fetched Oliver Pitcher's seven-pound axe out of his workshop near the cross where Oliver did his carpentry. His axes cut like razors and Ponto, followed by the youths, made for the gravestone in the churchyard. Another youth had been hiding under the ivy. He had just moved away when Ponto took one almighty swipe at it.

Our village didn't possess a bier and at funerals one had to be fetched from Beckford, two miles away. I shall always remember Ponto on the day of a funeral walking to Beckford and coming back along the road, drawing the four-wheeled truck which would be used to carry the coffin up the churchyard. Ponto never rode on this. He died in Evesham Workhouse and was buried in a pauper's grave.

CHAPTER EIGHT

SHEPHERD CORBISLEY AND HIS SHEEP

THE OLD SHEPHERD, as all the other men and boys on the farm called him, was one of nature's gentlemen, a man living very close to the soil and all living things except his fellow men. He only mixed at busy times; otherwise his life was lonely. It was considered an honour to help him out at his work and we boys looked upon him as something much more than a farm worker. There was something very stable about him and he seemed to have an inner peace and serenity which he had cultivated over the years. He was more or less his own boss over the sheep and his word was taken as law both by the other workers and usually by his employers.

A man born and bred on the Cotswolds, he seemed more at home on Bredon Hill than in the Vale. I can picture him in our granary on a winter's afternoon, stripped to the shirt, turning the cake crusher with which he ground the cotton and linseed cake slabs, or rather 'kibbled' it. Then he mixed together flaked maize, brewers grains and locust beans on the stone slab floor with a barn shovel. We used to pick out the locust beans and chew the pods which were sweet. 'Thur unt the goodness in this cake like thur used to be, Fred lad,' he said. 'They crushes it too hard and squeezes all the oil out on it.' I agreed but was out of my depth, being unable to compare this cake with cake years back.

When I read about Moses and the Prophets I thought of the shepherd and imagined them to be men like him. To be in his company, a jolly man with an infectious laugh, was my ambition at holiday times from school. He dressed for his job among sheep. His cord trousers were known as fall-fronted or broad falls, fastened up the sides like breeches with buttons. We called them tailboard front. He wore a corduroy waistcoat with lots of pockets, one for his watch; this was an old turnip watch, almost as big as a small clock. His thick silver watch chain had a golden sovereign on it. One pocket was for his tobacco tin and so on. In the other no doubt would be a tin of Stockholm tar and some raddle. His coat—when he wore it—was of dark-grey fustian, a hard-wearing cloth of heavy weft. I never saw him in anything else but an Oxford shirt with a blue stripe in it. Just below his knees he wore some leather straps called yorks. When I asked him what they were for he said, 'Oi, to kip the dust out of me eyes.' But I found out that their main purpose was to give the trousers a little fullness at the knee, and when he was sweating in the summertime and his clothes stuck to his body this would prevent his broad leather braces pulling the buttons off his trousers. At lambing time he wore something like a pinafore frock made of hurden or sacking tied with binder twine around his waist. When he wasn't smoking it, he stuck his clay pipe under the band of his battered trilby; and his crook (which I still use) completed his make-up. Well-dubbined hobnail boots, of course. I remember a car with dicky seat passed quickly through our village one day and the passenger in the dicky lost his trilby in the rough wind. The driver didn't stop and several people tried on this brand-new hat lying on the roadside. It fitted the shepherd best. On Sundays when he occasionally came to chapel I thought he looked a little like the Aga Khan; his features were distinguished.

On entering the Cross Barn lambing pen or the granary you could smell on him a mixture of Jeyes fluid, used to kill sheep maggots, or Stockholm tar, for healing wounds, twist tobacco, cider and sheep. Not that he wasn't clean. Mrs. Corbisley's washing was whiter than the driven snow that the shepherd sometimes had to dig his ewes out of on Bredon.

Dad was farming nearly five hundred acres in partnership with Mr. Harry Carter, and at about the end of every September they both went up into mid-Wales to buy some fresh Kerry ewes. These came by rail to Beckford Station about two miles away. I usually went with the shepherd and his dog Rosie to meet the train and drive the ewes home. As they came out of the truck he would watch them with a critical eye as the little puffs of blue smoke from his clay pipe rose into the September afternoon. It never seemed to rain on these occasions. 'They a bought a wrung un thur, Fred. Lumpy jaw.' As the ewes, glad to get out of the trucks, nibbled at the bit of grass in the station yard, the shepherd sized them up. 'They beunt a bad bunch, take um on the whole,' he would say, 'Thur's a lame un just come out. What did yer dad say they be? Three year olds?' Catching one with his crook he would open its mouth with the gentleness and manner of a dentist. 'That un a got six tith so hers three.' In those days ewes were what was known as 'got-up for sale', that is, they were coloured with a yellow ochre. The shepherd told me in a whisper, 'It's supposed to make um look bigger but it don't.' We moved the new flock very slowly. I walked in front, the shepherd and his dog behind. 'They ull soon want some water so we'll put them in the first ham by Carrants Brook.' That was the first of our grounds we reached. Shutting the gate, the shepherd and I walked about another half a mile home, when he told me all the good and bad points about his new charges. 'Thur's one or two of um, Fred, as looks as if they bin getting through the fences. They be craw-necked.' He meant by this that in squeezing through between stakes they had lost some wool off their necks. 'They beunt bad on thur fit. Only one lame and that ull be put right tomorrow. What we wants now is four good tups to put with them. I suppose yer Dad and Mr. Carter will be off to Gloucester, to Barton Fair on the 29th?' I said, 'Yes. I am going with them on the train.'

When we got to Barton Fair the rams were got up, as old Walt would say, like a dog's dinner. Squared across their back, the faces of the black-faced Suffolks gleamed with linseed oil, but Mr. Carter and Dad bought four Oxford Downs. They all had little halters on and though called ram lambs they looked grown up to me. At the Wessex for lunch the waitress came round: 'Roast beef, roast pork, boiled mutton or steak and kidney pie?' I plumped for the pie. Dad had roast beef, Mr. Carter roast pork. Mr. Carter always lived well and was generous on these trips. He and Dad often bought a piece of meat at a butcher's and took it to a restaurant to have it cooked while they waited, but we had a train to catch and rams to load today. 'Apple tart, plum tart, rice pudding?' said the waitress. Mr. Carter and I had apple tart. Dad, who suffered from indigestion, had the rice pudding. Both men being teetotal, Mr. Carter ordered three stone bottles of real Stone Ginger Beer.

There were always plenty in the market willing to take stock to the station near by. One bristly-chinned down-at-heel fellow smelling strongly of beer, begged the price of a cup of tea. 'Right,' said Dad. 'Give us a hand with these rams.' They were put in the guard's van of the passenger train we travelled in, tied up with their little halters. After Ginger had looked at his shilling and thought it ought to be more, the train moved off. We changed at Ashchurch and arrived at our little station at 5.20. Shepherd Corbisley was waiting on the platform with Bert, who had brought him down with Min in the milk float. The rams were loaded into the float once more under the shepherd's critical eye. 'Four smartish rams, Master,' the shepherd said, 'although I beunt all that keen on the one marked No. 3.' 'Why,' Mr. Carter said, 'he's a good long ram.' 'Oi, I knows all about that but thur's too much daylight under him.' What he was getting at was that he was a bit long in the leg and, the shepherd said, 'We don't want to breed no hurdle jumpers.'

We put the rams in the nag stable overnight and the shepherd filled a trough of water, and took them some nice sweet clover and a measure of his special mixture, cake, locust beans etc. Next morning I met the shepherd in the granary and he said, 'Have yu got a feow minutes to spare?' 'Yes,' I said. 'What is it you want?' 'Come and help me to raddle them tups in the nag stable.' He had mixed up raddle, a red powder with oil, in an old paint tin and made a flat spoon-shaped stick out of a piece of old ash hurdle bar, and he sat the rams up while I handed him the tin and the flat stick and he painted their flat breasts red until they had a covering of half an inch of red paste on them.

Now to drive four young rams half a mile to the ewes in the far ham would have been difficult so we brought the ewes along

to the sheep-pens in the yard. There were two hundred of them
and by the use of a special gate in the pens we got them into two
separate hundreds. Two rams were brought along and put with
each hundred ewes. One lot we drove up on to the leasow and
the other lot on to Paris Hill. The rams soon started work on
the 30th September. 'If we be alive and well we will be lambing
late in February,' the shepherd said. Every day or two he caught
the rams and raddled them. This went on for three weeks, then
he changed the colour to blue, and changed two rams from one
flock to the other and vice versa. By working in this way the
shepherd knew that the ones marked red would lamb first and
could part them at lambing time. Shakespeare said: 'Put a
young ram with an old ewe and you will get good results.' This
is what we were doing, a ram lamb and a three-year-old ewe.
The shepherd still had some of last year's lambs about waiting
to clear up the sprout stems on Bredon in the winter. He told
me once he had hurdled or penned his sheep on every mortal
thing on the farm bar the gillies (wallflowers). 'Sprouts, runner
beans, peas, cabbage, swedes and sparrowgrass.' 'Asparagus,
surely not, Shepherd,' I said. 'Oi, I have, Fred my boy. When
Master Carter and yer Dad grew their cabbage plants up between the newly-made beds of sparrowgrass, as usual they
didn't want half the plants so I took the ship along and grazed
um off. They be good scavengers, mind ya, but never give um
mangels till arter Christmas. Thur's no sugar in um.'

As lambing time approached the shepherd got busy thatching
hurdles, burra hurdles they were called locally, to make his
lambing pens in the big thatched Cross Barn. He had already
had two lambs in January. 'They was in lamb afore they came
here, mind,' he said. Walt was sent up to Great Hill on top of
Bredon with four horses and a waggon to fetch a load of sainfoin from a rick built up there that Job Barley had just started
for the strong store cattle ranging Spring Hill and Fuzz Hill.
Now there was never any hay made just right for the shepherd.
It was over-made, no better than barley straw, heated, mouldy,
no herbage in it, and when Walt unroped his waggon in the
Cross Barn, at the same time saying, 'How'll that do for tha,

Shepherd?', the shepher sniffed handfuls off the waggon. 'I a-sin better and I a-sin wuss,' the shepherd said.

Old Oliver was mending the wooden sheep troughs and smoothing them off with his draw knife. He was also making hay racks from withy all around the open yard where the ewes spent the night.

I was not officially allowed in the lambing pen. We were not supposed to know the facts of life or death at such an early age. But there were ways and means of getting into the old Cross Barn and watching the shepherd act as midwife, doctor, and sometimes as undertaker, sexton and high priest. Sheep, as Job Barley remarked, won't stand punishment as a cow will. The shepherd never reckoned to take his clothes off during lambing but Dad took over every day from five o'clock tea-time until 10.30 at night, when the old shepherd had a nap on the sofa at home. He left his dog with Mrs. Corbisley at night and I have been with him coming away from his house when he said to his dog Rosie, 'Now look arter her, mind.'

One year our ewes had liver fluke very badly and a lot of them died. The shepherd said to me, 'When they have got a lump under thur jaw and goes glassy-eyed it's soon all over.' The shepherd got very upset about losing so many ewes. He talked of jumping in the moat when he fetched his money one Friday night. Dad said, 'We're not blaming you. It's bad all over the country.' The shepherd added that he didn't mind carrying any tool about with him, however heavy, 'but not this yer spade.' I agree that it's very disheartening burying animals which have died from disease.

Dad had bought twenty ewes from near Stratford. The shepherd never liked them—they were Oxfords. But they made up a bunch. Every time a ewe died the shepherd would say, 'It's one of them you bought from by Stratford, Master.' I well remember after a time Dad saying, 'Bless the man, I should think they must be all dead by now. I saw the old man Corbisley put four in one grave in the orchard one February morning.'

There was sainfoin in the rick on Great Hill. Another boy and I used to smoke the heads, which were like clover, in clay

pipes on Sundays. I wouldn't recommend it. It made our eyes
run and our throats sore.

When the lambs were big enough, the wind was in the right
direction, and the shepherd had a convenient day, they had to
have their tails cut and the male lambs were castrated. This was
done in the Cross Barn. He used a bone-handled knife, as old
as himself and very sharp, to cut the lambs' tails. Bert usually
held the lambs. I wasn't 'hardly mon enough', the shepherd
said. The ram lambs were held by Bert by all four legs, the lamb
resting against Bert's chest. The shepherd cut off the purse,
then he leaned forward, drew the stones out with the few teeth
he had left, and dropped them in a bucket. All the time he
chewed twist tobacco and spat in the wound he made in each
ram lamb. Just imagine the scene—the shepherd's whiskers and
moustache stained with twist tobacco and blood; the lambs—
well, the ewe lambs didn't bother much running off minus their
tails, but the ram lambs, suffering from shock, sometimes lay
still for a few seconds before rushing out of the back door of the
barn, where the Peagood Nonesuch apple trees and the Pitmaston Duchess pears were now in full bloom. The tails and
sweetbreads were cooked by Mrs. Corbisley and it's possible that
the butcher didn't have to call that week.

Now he generally left about twenty or so of the late lambs
until they got a bit bigger. I can hear now the conversation on
Friday night in our court-yard when he fetched his money.
'Shepherd, don't you think you ought to cut those other few
lambs Monday?' The shepherd said, 'They beunt hardly big
enough, Master. Give um another wick.' We all knew that by
that time old shepherd would have a better meal from them, but
who could blame him?

On Saturday afternoons the shepherd could be found in his
garden by his potato and beetroot bury with a pair of steel-
rimmed glasses perched at the end of his nose, while several
villagers waited their turn with their wicker baskets holding
young tom-cats. He looked quite a professional man as he per-
formed this delicate operation. (I won't go into details; enough
to say that although Shepherd Corbisley had not got

M.R.C.V.S. at the end of his name he was a highly successful cat doctor.) I never knew one go wrong.

What a colourful character this man was and such a devoted couple, he and his wife!

I helped him many times in the hayfields and I shall never forget one ketchy haymaking, when three-quarters of the rick was up by tea and Mr. Carter had just bought a wireless set, which forecast rain. Dad and Mr. Carter looked at another field of hay almost ready and decided to pick it up after tea. The old shepherd was furious. 'It unt gwain to rain with the wind where it is. The hay is never fit in this wide world. It'll fire as safe as eggs.' The shepherd continued to build the rick and it was finished off by night. Then came the big job of getting the old man down the ladder. As he put his trembling hand on the top of the ladder Dad, who was on the rick with him, held his other arm, while another man stood on the bottom round of the forty-round ladder, and then one foot at a time the shepherd descended. When he reached the ground he said, 'Thur, I udn't go up on that rick again for five pounds.' After a few days, as the men arrived at seven o'clock in the early morning mist, the rick had a sickly hot smell and steam would rise. The old man, with his bronchial laugh, would say, 'Look you at the rick. It'll fire.' It didn't fire but got very hot and the middle came out a dark brown like the shepherd's twist.

He built the straw rick thatching and one year I was carrying water to the steam engine, which is not a full-time job, so Dad said, 'Go and help the shepherd on the straw rick.' As I moved the boltings to him he said, 'This straw won't do for thatching. It's knocked about too much with these new machines. Thur was nothing like the 'ooden drum to turn out a straight bolting. They never knocked the straw about so much.' This machine we were using was about thirty years old but the shepherd was a die-hard. Then he told me of driving the bullocks at plough on the Cotswolds as a boy and how they used to catch a bree fly and put a horsehair round it and tie it, then put it by the bullock's ear. The bullock's tail would go straight up and it would run away with the plough. I said, 'Shepherd boys will be boys.' He then told me of a threshing machine getting stuck in a wet rickyard. The horses couldn't move it and kept breaking the tackle. The bullock ploughman said, 'Let me put a couple of my bullocks on and move it,' and everyone was surprised when the bullocks pulled together, so steadily, and moved the machine.

He was always game to sing at a concert and his little item at the Armistice Tea is worth remembering. The chairman, who was sometimes Dad, would say, 'What about you, Shepherd?' 'I got it on my chest tonight, Master,' he replied. His wife said, 'Come on. You can manage a couple.' Of his first I can only remember a few lines but it went like this:

> 'She was sixteen stone, all muscle and bone;
> Then she feel into a decline through
> swallowing a mouse in her beer.'

Next was:

> The Fox and the Hare,
> The Badger and the Bear,
> And the Birds in the Greenwood Tree,
> The Pretty Little Rabbit,
> So engaged in his habit;
> You have all got a mate but me.

Quick-witted and kindly, the old shepherd was the salt of the earth. I visited him the night before he died and he was still very much up with what was going on. A man from Shipston way had said that he mowed an acre a day in his orchard and he was over seventy. (This was a report in the local paper the shepherd was reading.) 'The old liar,' he said. 'Who's a gwain to believe that? Every tree you come to you have a hindrance. Very different from mowing an acre of open ground.' I had a pleasant hour with him, as he joked on the bed. 'It's me water,' he said. 'I expect it'll finish me.' Weeks before I had taken at his request agrimony flowers for him to drink the tea.

When we buried him up at the churchyard on a day of thunder and rain, following a hot spell, I could feel the tears streaming down my cheeks as I remembered such a dear old friend.

CHAPTER NINE

JASPER

JASPER HILL was a member of a family which had lived in our village since the seventeenth century. Tall and lean, he always looked the same, and seemed a fairly old man when I was a boy; yet he lived into the 1960s to the ripe old age of ninety. When he was seventy-odd he worked for me for two years but had been a coalman a lot of his life.

To say his wife Emma was careful would be an understatement. They lived on the bare minimum. Emma was a great believer in pastry lard—in fact, anything that was cheap. That and bread pudding was their staple diet. Jasper brought this for his mid-morning bait, washed down with cold tea without milk or sugar. Emma used to come as charwoman to our house. She had no breakfast before she came but had a cup of cocoa and plenty of bread and cheese at our house for lunch. She worked on the land in the afternoon, doing anything in season such as gilly (wallflower) picking and onion and asparagus tying, and when the sprout stems from the previous year's picking had gone dry and hard in the stacks in the corner of the field she took some home every night in her blue and white cotton apron to burn under the boiler to do her washing. Soap she rarely bought but took home in a little bag all the bits we had left as too small to use. Dr. Overthrow told Jasper to drink plenty of barley water. Emma boiled the same barley twice. She said all the strength didn't come out first time.

One of the three pleasures enjoyed in life was riding his bike. He had the same one for thirty years and got on a step on the hub of the back wheel. After a lot of scuffling and scooting he heaved himself into the saddle and was away. A lot of the older men got on their bikes by the step. The step jutted out about three inches long on the left side of the bike. The rider straddled the back wheel, putting his left foot on the step, scooted with his right one until the correct speed was reached to hold the bike steady, then up and over. Jasper's bike always shone and looked new; when he came in to tea Emma made him rub it over with an oily rag and hang it from the beams in his cottage before he was allowed to have his meal. If the day had been wet he had to give it a real good clean. Walt used to tell him, just to pull his leg, 'I should like to borrow thy bike tonight, Jasper. I got to go down to Beckford.' He didn't have to wait long for his answer. 'I specks not,' Jasper said. 'The missis won't let me lend him nobody.'

Football he was fond of and attended matches within cycling distance. He was at a match at Alderton one Saturday when a heavy storm came on rather suddenly. Jasper took off his top coat, covered his bike up and got wet through. Walt told him, 'Thee uds't never ketch cold. Thee bist too fulla pastry lard.'

At ordinary league matches in the Wynch there was no admission charge but at half time one of the committee went round with the box. Jasper, everyone noticed, kept his hands in his pockets almost up to his elbows as the wooden box was rattled in front of him. For hospital cup finals, semi-finals, etc., threepence was charged at the stile by the horse pond for admittance. Now Jasper's garden ran right down to the football field in the Wynch and at the bottom of the garden just over the little low hedge was his one Victoria plum tree. To save threepence on these rare occasions Jasper climbed this tree and viewed the match from there. Some of the village lads knew all about his little scheme and on the Saturday dinner-time before one cup final got some ticky-tack or banding grease and plastered Jasper's tree. How he got this off his trousers and what Emma said I don't know. Some of Jasper's comments at the home matches were a bit off-beat, and the referee was always wrong. You could hear old Jasper's comments: 'How's he for offside, Ref? Dos't want to borrow my glasses?' He wore a pair of steel-rimmed ones well down his nose.

At cricket he liked to see a bit of action and if the runs didn't come quickly you would hear him. 'Mind thee doesn't break that bat.' 'They don't hit out like they used to years ago.' He was always reminding me of years ago. 'This or that udn't a done in the Squire's time years ago.' In 1888, he said, 'it started freezing in November and we had sixteen wick's frost in February!' I said: 'That must have been a long February.' He said: 'It was that. I never done no work all the winter except a wick or two's threshing.' I said: 'How did you manage?' Jasper said: 'We a'most lived on boiled swedes and taters and me and thee Uncle Jim at Christmas walked all round Bredon Hill with a melodeon and went carol-singing to the big houses. Some gen us vittle,' he said, 'Others drink or money. About the end a March the weather took up and me and thee Uncle George went wheat hoeing and we had a beautiful spring.'

He was a handy man hoeing and the last job he did for me was to chop the mangolds out or single them. He must have had a constitution like a horse. As Walt said, 'If thee was to have a good meal a grub it ud kill tha.'

When he and Emma married it was on the rebound. Jasper had been courting Emma's sister and his words 'she chocked him up one Sunday night after chapel.' He said, 'Thee knowst where that little Sally Coppice is a-thine next to the 'ood?' I said, 'Yes, where the bluebells grow.' 'Well,' said Jasper. 'I took her up as fur as thur one Sunday night after chapel. Thee knowst whur that stile is at the bottom as goes into the barn ground?' I said, 'Yes, of course I do.' 'Well, what do you think her said to me after I had took her up thur? He said, 'Jasper, I don't wish to keep company with you any more." What dost think a that? Fanny her name was and her had bin out along uth Ern Johnson, mind tha. Her told me as how Ern Johnson had put his hand on her knee. "I don't know what his intentions were," she said.' Jasper said, 'Oi. I knowed though.'

When Fanny broke off with Jasper, they had already had the banns published, or 'bin asked in church'. The next couple to be asked in church was Jasper and Emma, Fanny's sister, just a few weeks after. When he got married he was working as carter on the Squire's farm and his work-mates teased him. 'They reckoned that I was obliged to but I knowed different. Just two years,' he said, 'afore the missis had the fust babby. Do you know what the gaffer (that was the Squire's bailiff) said? He said. "That un a bin a long while on the way, Jasper".' He said, 'It's all right. I knowed different.'

One winter the Squire's bailiff gave Jasper permission to have some swedes. Fetching some one moonlight night he met the man he always referred to as 'the bobby'. 'I dare say thee thoughtst thee hadst got a capture,' said Jasper. 'Well, thee asn't then cos I got orders to fetch what I wants to.' 'No,' said the policeman. 'I just wondered who was about the swede field this hour of the night.' The following night Jasper was riding his bike from Beckford without lights long after lighting-up time. 'I got a capture tonight, Jasper,' the policeman said, as he stepped out from behind the hedge.

Going into his living room one Friday tea-time to ask him to come on the Monday and give a hand at threshing, I automatically took off my cap. 'Thee hadst no cause to take thee hat off, Fred lad. We beunt proud folks in yur.' It was rather gloomy inside the cottage. The windowsills were full of white geraniums which, as Job Barley, our cowman, said, 'had bin thur since the remembrance of mon', the floor was covered with newspaper to keep Jasper's hobnails off the scraps of lino. I noticed one window sealed up with paper and mentioned to Jasper, 'I should get a piece of glass and some putty and mend it.' 'Why should I spend my money on other folks' property?' came his reply quick, and to the point. 'Well,' I said, if you prefer the draught.' The green-tasselled tablecloth was also partly covered with paper. 'I see you have a Sunday paper,' I said, rather surprised at the outlay. 'Oi,' he said, 'we do but the missis won't let me read him till Monday.' It was a popular one and Jasper's mind was not to be corrupted on Sunday, as he sat on the blue stone slab which formed a covering to the stand-pipe tap on the grass verge opposite his cottage.

Jasper's wife would not allow him to smoke or drink, but on his coal round he would treat himself, when he got a tip, to a packet of cigarettes. He kept these in his saddle bag of his bike. His wife found them and he was really on the carpet. The fellows at work who knew about it used to put their butt ends in Jasper's saddle bag because Emma searched it every night when he came home. She would say, 'Jasper, you have been smoking again,' and, poor old chap, he had a hard job to convince his wife what really had happened when she searched his saddle bag.

One Christmas Jasper won a bottle of port wine in a draw. Mother said to Emma, 'What will you do with it? You don't drink.' 'We have a tablespoonful each before we go to bed,' said Emma, 'just for medicine.'

As I have said, Jasper was always on about the past. 'Things be different to what they was years ago.' Meet him any fine day, say in February or March, and the conversation would be something like this: 'Good morning. Jasper. Quite a nice morning this morning.' 'So you might think,' he would reply. 'It's a weather breeder. Now listen to what I gwain to tell tha. We shall have to suffer for this later on. We shall like enough get some frosts in May.'

Among other things he grew in his garden was rhubarb which he was very proud of. He never gave much away. It was rumoured that he had had a good hiding as a boy for giving another boy something. One day as I was passing he was sitting in his usual place on the stone slab over the tap. He said 'Shouldst like a bit a rhubarb?' 'Yes, just enough to make a pie.' Jasper gave it me and I said, 'What good rhubarb it is,' and he said, 'I'll let tha into a little secret. We allus empties the closet bucket on it.' I'm afraid that put me off Jasper's rhubarb.

He was walking down to church one Sunday with his stick with a horse's head handle which he had won at hoopla at Ashton Club. It was ten minutes to one. I said, 'Where you off so late, Jasper?' He said, 'To church. It wants about ten minutes to eleven.' Someone had told him to put the clocks back an hour instead of forward. He had no wireless. 'I did know we had to put um forrard this time,' he said, and he went home to get a late dinner. Another time a friend met him as he went to church and told him it was very necessary for him to go, as he was a big sinner. 'No wus than anybody else,' he said, 'and besides it yunt allus them as goes to church and chapel as goes to heaven.'

We hope he's resting there. He was an interesting character in our village. Apart from his coal-heaving, he scratched the top six inches of some of the farmland around Ashton for nearly eighty years.

CHAPTER TEN

STOCKY HILL

STOCKY HILL, as he was called in the village, was Jasper's elder brother and lived in a cottage next door. He was a bachelor then, a terrific worker able to cut an acre of wheat in a day with the two hooks, but he was more noted for his digging the heavy clay soil of the village. A chain or four hundred and eighty-four square yards with an Evesham Two Tine or two-prong digger didn't come amiss to him. Job Barley, our cowman, used to describe him as a stomachful. He didn't mean Stocky was awkward, but that he could not give in or give up a job. There was nothing one would notice about his appearance in the late twenties. Wearing a black kind of beaver hat, cord waistcoat and cord trousers, both of washed-out fawn, he was upright, broad-shouldered, a man who looked full of work yet. He was named Stocky for obvious reasons, Jasper, his brother, being head and shoulders taller.

He had a face which fairly bristled with whiskers, the beard kept fairly short. He smoked a pipe, usually a clay one, and the pleasant scent of Red Bell Shag on a frosty morning as he passed our house was in keeping with the countryside, the birds, the flowers, and between the high-banked hedges of our lane it lingered in a blue-grey cloud. Like Stocky, a part of nature itself.

Despite the mature, rugged look of this village Hampden he started courting at about sixty-five a servant girl of doubtful age from Cheltenham. Stocky used to take her back towards the big house in Cheltenham where she worked, walking with her to the Farmers Arms nearly at Bishops Cleeve. She pushed her bike and these Sunday nights Stocky walked about fifteen miles. In his own words he said, when he kissed her goodnight, 'That rattled just like a whip a-smacking!' On her days off Stocky and Ada did a part of their courting down the snaky, wandering lane known as Back Lane or Gipsies Lane.

Stocky was a man of few words. No wonder he had started courting very late in life and he had to learn. 'Why dosn't say summat?' Ada said one night. (The boys had followed them to catch every word.) 'What be I to say?' said Stocky. 'Why dosn't say as you loves me?' 'So I do,' said Stocky. Ada followed up with, 'Don't the stars shine bright tonight?' 'Oi, they do,' replied Stocky.

This unusual courtship went on for some time and they thought of marriage. Stocky spoke to the vicar, who asked him the name of the lucky girl. 'Ada,' said Stocky. The vicar said, 'I know that. What I want to know is her surname.' 'Lor bless the fella I couldn't tell tha. I allus calls her darling,' Stocky said in a rather superior tone. The vicar sorted things out and then trouble started. The Hill family thought it was a very unsatisfactory union and refused to have anything more to do with Stocky Hill. The old chap was furious, brought his bag of sixty golden sovereigns down to the village cross and, with the youths egging him on, said he had decided to broadcast his money there and then and throw it to anyone, then go and jump into the moat. 'Go on, Stocky, show um you means business,' they told him, but he put his money back in his inside poacher's pocket of his Derby tweed jacket, and walked up to the moat, the lads egging him on and saying, 'Show um you means business.'

There was no broadcasting of Stocky's sovereigns and he didn't jump in the moat but the following Sunday morning in our village church Edward Hill and Ada Styles were asked in church for the first time. Stocky was persuaded to go and when his name was read out he said in a loud stage whisper, 'Lors, that made I sweat,' mopping his brow with a clean red and white spotted handkerchief.

The wedding day arrived but Stocky was not an easy man to marry. When the vicar popped the question he answered 'Yes' instead of 'I will.' 'You must say "I will", Mr. Hill,' the vicar insisted, and Stocky came out with 'All right then, if that's it, I will.'

At the lichgate at the bottom of the churchyard and at the village cross quite a handful of people had gathered to wish this odd couple well. But Stocky and Ada were signing the register and Milly Bosworth was playing suitable pieces on the organ. Stocky could not sign his name, only mark a cross. Stocky and Ada did not come out of the church door, through the porch and down the churchyard. 'Oh no, my boy,' as Stocky told me later. 'I knowed they was a-waiting for us down in that lichgate with their rice and their 'fetti so me and the missis come out of the back vestry door and took the footpath across the field to the cottage.' The vicar asked Stocky about the honeymoon. Stocky said, 'Bless the fellow. We've already had that on Fuzz Hill.'

After the wedding they settled down happily but Stocky was always in evidence if there was an election, firmly believing that things didn't go off as they should if there was no fighting, and he would try and start something of the sort for old times' sake, remembering the rowdy elections of his youth.

When Stocky died the vicar told Ada, 'You have been a mother to him besides being a wife.'

CHAPTER ELEVEN

JOE BAKER AND WATER DIVINING

I HAVE ALWAYS been intrigued by the mysterious and by mysteries. There is something in delving into things which can't be handled that gives a certain satisfaction. Water divining is a gift—you have either got it or you haven't. Joe Baker was a mystic. He was a water diviner extraordinary. 'Some folks thinks I have got a tile loose,' he told me one day. 'Just because I have learnt a few things without ever rubbing my back against a college wall.'

A nearby small town was short of water and Joe Baker said there was any amount up on Spring Hill, about three-quarters of the way up Bredon. One Saturday afternoon in mid-winter Joe, accompanied by Dad, Mr. Carter and me, started to climb the hill with one object in view, to find enough water to supply the small nearby town. We all knew the springs which flowed constantly out of the mounds covered with rough wiry grass on the northern slopes of Spring Hill, but Joe said there was also an underground stream on the south side. When I said he was a water diviner extraordinary, what I meant was that he did not use a forked stick and hold the two-forked end to find water. He had copper wires around his arm and from these he suspended a pendulum made from the golden top of an umbrella filled with mercury. When he was standing over a subterranean stream the golden knob rotated in a certain way.

We walked through Paris gardens, a hamlet on the lower slopes, past the barn and up on to the Leasows, where Mr. Carter bowled over a rabbit with his twelve bore. It was started from a blackberry bush just to the left of the middle gateway by Dingo, a little Pomeranian dog, who would face any thorns where rabbits lay. Mr. Carter paunched and hocked the rabbit and gave it me to carry. Mr. Carter and Dad both had their guns; in fact, they never went on the hill without them. We reached Spring Hill at about three o'clock and Joe Baker got ready his dangler, as he called it. From the Leasow gateway he followed the horse road for about a hundred and fifty yards and nothing happened with his strange device. He then made a sharp left-hand turn towards Grafton Firs and soon the golden knob began to rotate, slowly at first, then gathering momentum until Joe stopped almost on his knees on a knoll near a few hawthorn trees, stunted by the poorness of the ground. As Joe stood there trembling he explained that it was taking energy from his body and he had to restrict his divining to allow him to get back this energy.

He told Mr. Carter and Dad that he would not advise sinking a well there and that there were better places ahead. In single file with me bringing up the rear, we followed this imaginary water course for about two hundred yards, Joe Baker sometimes walking in circles and sometimes in almost a straight line. When the water was near the surface Joe was brought to his knees and the golden ball rotated like a seat in one of the chairplanes that I had seen at the Mop.

In a hollow shaped like a basin, at the foot of a steep bank alive with rabbits, Joe stopped a long time. 'Thousands of gallons of clear spring water,' he said, 'are pouring under my feet, quite shallow too. Now if you want to dig to find plenty to supply the small town on the other side of the hill, there is abundant water here, and with the two springs on the northern slope a reservoir could be made.' We were about eight hundred feet above sea level so there would have been no difficulty about fall, the town that was so short of water being on the River Avon. Both Dad and Mr. Carter were now almost as sure as Joe that by just digging down a few feet the water would just gush out from this stream yet unseen and the exact quantity in gallons per minute a speculation. I just stood there, a raw youth with a rabbit, expecting at any time to see rabbits produced from hats. I said nothing, just listened. 'What about it, Tom?' Mr. Carter said to Dad. 'Shall we send old Oliver and Taffy up Monday morning and start to sink a shaft?' 'All right, Harry,' Dad said to Mr. Carter, 'but they will want some timber before they get too deep.' Mr. Carter said, 'Right. We'll send Walt with a muck-cart and two horses to take their tackle up.' Now up until now Joe Baker had been successful in finding water in several villages round the Vale with his dangler.

Monday morning came, and as it was the school holiday I went with Walt and the horses and cart, and took Oliver's and Taffy's tools and timber up to the basin-shaped hollow on Spring Hill. Instead of digging a round well-shaped hole they dug a square shaft and struck the Cotswold limestone only inches under the turf. With pick axes and shovels, spades and grafts, they pressed on. First there was a layer of stone, then shale and gravel as hard-packed as rock. When they came to a very large stone they dug round it, loosened it with their crow-bars and then hauled it up on a rope.

The latter end of January, when I was back at school, Taffy who had pale blue eyes which fairly sparkled when he looked up out of the deepening, now well-timbered shaft, came to our bow window overlooking the courtyard where Dad paid out the wages every Friday night. It was about seven o'clock in the evening and I was doing my homework by the light of an oil lamp hanging from our living-room ceiling. There was a knock at the back door and I went to open the middle of the bow window with a candle in my hand. This saved me a few yards to the door. Taffy's eyes sparkled in the light of the candle but I had seen nothing yet. 'I say, mun, can I see your father quickly? We have struck gold on Spring Hill.' I ran back into the kitchen where Dad was reading *The Echo* and told him to hurry up and see Taffy. He had struck gold. Out of his jacket he brought out several nuggets about the size of cricket balls which sparkled in the candlelight even more than Taffy's eyes. Dad said, 'It looks like some sort of gold to me. Fred, take one piece to school in the morning and ask the chemistry master.'

That night, as we sat around our old oven grate in the kitchen and one after another handled these nuggets, I thought of what I had read of the Klondike and the Gold Rush and whether anything of the sort would or could happen here. That night I could hardly sleep with excitement. I had been entrusted with the task of finding out the truth.

On the 8.50 a.m. train out of our village station I met the usual school friends and told them what I had in my satchel. 'Let's just have a look at it before you show it to Dapper,' they said. I unbuckled my satchel and undid the brown paper parcel and the nugget was handed around the carriage.

We didn't have chemistry that day so I had to catch Dapper at break. 'Please, sir,' I said, 'could you tell me what this is?' One look and he said, 'Fools' gold—copper pyrites. Where did you find it, Archer?' I told him it was about fifteen feet down a shaft on Bredon. 'It's no good,' he said. 'Very common.' I kept it for a bit along with other junk in my drawer hoping he was wrong.

At twenty feet down the shaft there was still no sign of water and Dad got a bit tired of Taffy and Oliver digging up there when they could have been hedge-cutting and fencing, their usual winter jobs, and the dig was called off. Joe Baker, naturally disappointed, used to take his dangler down the shaft and round and round it went, faster than ever. We shall never know whether if they had dug perhaps only another six feet into the now fairly solid rock, the much sought-after water would have oozed out and make Taffy and Oliver beat a hasty retreat.

Joe Baker, besides being able to divine water, claimed also to be able to find coal, salt and human skeletons. He used to practise on the last up in the churchyard. He had other fandangos, as Job Barley, our cowman, called them, for divining which rang little bells. I shall never forget how he demonstrated at a local flower show and said there was oil underneath an orchard. One local old labourer who had had one too many tots of cider, said. 'What sort of oil is it? Hair oil?' On one of our Sunday school outings to Barry, Joe sat in the back seat with some of his equipment. We were travelling in our village twenty-seater bus. As the bus took us past Gloucester, Chepstow and beyond, Joe could be heard every so often: 'My word, there's some water here.' Then, 'Now we are over coal' or 'oil' or whatever the bell rang for. We enjoyed this part of the outing quite as much as the fun-fair and candy-floss of Barry.

Joe was a man of many parts. He could be very serious when he taught us at Sunday school. He had been a shepherd as a young man and told us of the Good Shepherd, 'I often wonder,' he would say, 'what will become of you boys when you grow into men. Now don't get swelled-headed when you are fourteen and think you are men and too old to come here,' he'd say. He used to tell us of the dire poverty of his boyhood. His father was a drunkard and treated his wife and children very badly. He recalled how he drove oxen to plough on Bredon at ten years of age. He had no jacket, just a sack over his shoulders, and with hands raw with chilblains he washed in the morning at the roadside tap in icy water. 'Fred lad,' he told me, 'my father used to play the fiddle round the pubs for drink but he hung the fiddle up at our door and beat my poor mother.' He said, 'Never hang your fiddle up at the door,' which I thought was good advice. 'I could take you to a cottage,' he said, 'where one wall is marked with bacon fat where my father threw the frying pan at mother in a drunken bout.'

Joe learned to read and write from his wife after he married. He learned to read the Bible and knew it very well. He talked a lot about Job, how he scraped the sores off his body with a ploughshare. To an extent, I suppose, Joe Baker had suffered as a boy like Job.

Joe Baker played the big bass viol at chapel and had a mellow bass singing voice. He could remember the orchestra playing the music from the church gallery. At concerts and social evenings Joe would give an exhibition with the bones to piano accompaniment. He also played the tin whistle and recited:

'I comes up from the country but I beunt so very green.
I knows that two and two be four and twice four beunt
    eighteen.
I reads a lot of things in books. I learned a bit at school.
Folks tries to do me but I does they. Because I looks a fool.'

At the evening chapel meeting he was not on the plan but

took the place of a preacher who failed to turn up. 'Stop-gap Baker, that's me. I'm here to stand in the breach.'

He was unequalled as a grafter of fruit trees. Somewhere between ninety and a hundred per cent of them grew. He did it the only way common in his time, plastering the joint with puddled blue clay after he had tied his grafts in with raffia. As a pruner of trees he was an authority and some nicely balanced trees today are the result of his training.

When he was gardener up at the Hurst he became well known for his roses. I also remember him turfing lawns. He had a turfing iron which shone like silver. Then he beat the turf into shape with a home-made tool like a flat square beetle.

What couldn't Joe Baker do? The only thing I didn't see him do was to thatch a rick. He could build one. It's a pleasure for me to cast my mind back not so many years and see in my mind's eye Joe Baker, with a straw boater covered with a net, his face covered, his hands gloved, a straw skep in his hand, going out on a June evening to take a swarm of bees. He kept many hives of bees and when they swarmed in all sorts of odd places, Joe Baker would take them.

One summer's evening, Mr. Carter, some of the men and young Bert Bradfield were coming down Bredon after a hard day's work among the sainfoin, pitching and loading the wag-gon and ricking it by the Great Hill Barn. On the Barn Hill, which had not been cut for hay, Bert, who had eyes like a hawk, spotted something shaped like a rugby football on top of a large boar thistle. 'Master Carter,' he said, 'yer's a swarm of bees.' 'My boy,' said Mr. Carter, 'tell Joe Baker when you get home and bring him up and help him to take them. I expect he will give you a shilling.' Bert did as Mr. Carter advised him to and came up late that evening with Joe and they took the swarm. 'Master Carter said you'd give me a shilling, Master Baker, but I beunt a-going to axe you for it.' Joe Baker said, 'Oh ah.' He didn't give him the shilling but did one better. He paid his fare for a day trip to Weston-super-Mare the following week.

Joe was a man of principle. As he told us at Sunday school, if a man asks you to go a mile, go two. Whether he was laying a hedge, building a rick, budding a rose or grafting, you could depend the job was done right. There was no need to find any tools for him. He had a tool for every job he did. Today I passed a Pitmaston Duchess pear tree that Joe grafted on a hawthorn tree many many years ago. He died getting on for twenty years more than the allotted span and worked until his end, which was peace.

CHAPTER TWELVE

ROUGH CARPENTRY, RABBIT ING
AND THE HUMAN SKULL

OLIVER HAMPTON, a bachelor, lived in a little thatched cottage, now known as Rookery Nook but then as the Cross, lodging with my Auntie Phoebe. At right angles to the cottage and following the bend in the road was an old tumbledown barn, at one time Dick Miles's wheelwright's shop. Oliver, by various tricks of rough carpentry, had saved the barn from falling down and used a part of it for his workshop. Many a pleasant summer evening I have spent in there with Oliver sitting on his chopping block and watching him make or mend some odd tool or other. From wooden pegs sticking out from the wall hung ladders of all lengths.

Oliver, full of humour (he just couldn't be sarcastic), called me 'Foreman' (I was a boy of ten or eleven). At home it was my job every evening to take the wood basket through the long stone-slabbed passages of our old house and grope my way by the light of a candle until I reached the coal- and wood-house and there cut the sticks for lighting the fire in our kitchen next morning. The oven grate was the only means of boiling the kettle so the first kettle had to be boiled by sticks alone and the small coal placed around the kettle which hung from a chain and pot hook.

Oliver knew all about this and often said, 'How's that hatchet a yours, Foreman?' 'Getting a bit blunt, Oliver,' I replied. 'Bring him along tonight arter tay. We'll touch him up a bit.' Oliver after tea looked very dubiously at my little hatchet, which he described as being 'as blunt as a plough coulter' and that 'anybody could a'mus ride barebacked to London on him avout being cut'. 'But afore we has him on the grindstun I'll put a fresh stick in for ya.' Now besides ladders in Oliver's place were pieces of wood in various stages of seasoning: larch poles for ladder-making, red withy for ladder rounds (or rungs), ash for axe helves, shuppick stales and rabbit-wire pegs.

Oliver was a little bent man and he needed to be. The roof was low as if it was almost built to fit him. As his eyes wandered around the apparent junk, wood shavings, sawdust, gate hooks and the like, he was looking for a straight piece of ash about fifteen to eighteen inches long to make a new helve for my little hatchet. 'Yur's a bit, Foreman, out of the Sally Coppice up at Kersoe, as tough as any thunk.' (Thunk was the rawhide thongs used to join threshing machine belts, etc.) Into the vice it went and Oliver, first with draw knife then spoke shave, moulded it into a handle for my little hatchet. His tools cut like razors and as he sharpened them with his whetstones of different kinds I sat there intrigued, thinking 'This is no rough carpenter.' All the time he chewed twist tobacco, which became evident as he moistened with spittle the various whetstones.

With a saw he made a cut at the head end of the helve to drive a wedge in. He then tapped the head gently on and with his wooden mallet hit the other end of the handle until the head was in place. Into the vice and in went the wedge. A rub over with sandpaper and then a linseed-oil-soaked rag and the job was complete. 'How's that, Foreman? Now let's have him on the grindstun.' I turned and Oliver soon made a cutting edge on the blunt blade. Now more rubbing on the blue-coloured whetstone, more spittle, more twist tobacco.

Oliver's talents were varied but I think he liked working in wood the best. He mended our gates, put shafts on waggons, horse rolls, did a bit of bricklaying, and was an expert at the dying art of dry-stone walling. About July every year his evenings were spent making pegs for rabbit wires. These he made from cleft ash, dry and seasoned. They are best described as tent pegs in miniature. These were driven into the ground with a mallet made from crab-apple wood with an ash handle made by Oliver. The pegs held the snares of copper wire by a short cord fixed to them by a slip knot. The oval-shaped snares which Oliver set in the rabbit runs were propped about two inches off

the ground by a small nut stick with a groove or slit in the top
called a pertch peg. Oliver cut these pegs from the nut bushes
alongside the path to our privy in the back garden.

The rabbits on Bredon were strong and weighty and often
broke the factory-made wires which were woven from six
strands of plain brass wire. Oliver made his own. Suspended
from a beam in his workshop he hung eight, not six, strands of
wire, and with a lead weight at the bottom he spun this round
and made his wires threading the one end through a small eye
he fixed in the other. What would shine more brightly on a
moonlight night than copper or brass, new and gleaming?
'They won't wear them necklaces until I faked um a bit,' he told
me. This he did by making a fire of wood shavings and smoking
the wires until the shiny newness had gone.

Let's think of his ladders, all hand-made. There were his sixty-
rung for walnut picking and roof repairs, and his forty-rung for
picking the Pitmaston Duchess pears in the Cross Barn orchard
or for putting bolt upright against the end of a hayrick. He
made unusual ladders with a slight curve, about fifteen rungs, so
that the man unloading a load of hay or corn could get on the
waggon and once he was up there give the ladder a push to fall
on the ground out of the way. The slight curve, or cant, as
Oliver called it, saved it from breaking as it fell like a boom-
erang. Short ladders he made for cottagers to hang their pig
carcasses on, to await cutting-up next day. He once made a
short ladder for blackberrying, about eight rounds long, so that
his niece could reach the best berries on top of the hedges. But
Oliver liked to tell me of Tommy Dyke and his watercress ladder. 'Three rungs,' he said, 'and he stood on the middle un.'

From October until early March every year Oliver's main job
was rabbiting. He and Mr. Carter set the wires and I followed
behind with the crab-apple wood mallet and drove the pegs in.
They both set these snares almost as fast as they could walk and
we usually kept in a straight line across the fields in order that
they could be looked at at night. A lot has been said and written
about the kindest way to kill a rabbit. Undoubtedly the cruellest
is the gin trap. I never cared for trapping and we did very little.

The stoat, the rabbit's natural enemy, can be very tantalising. The shot-gun can cripple and maim. Ferreting varies so much depending on conditions, depth of the holts or holes, that it's difficult to generalise. Gassing is cowardly, and my humble opinion is that the wire snare, regularly visited, is the most humane.

With the aid of a carbide cycle lamp I went up Bredon with Oliver and Mr. Carter in the dark winter's evenings to look around the wires. Now old Oliver, who probably knew more about the lie of the land this side of the hill than anyone, took short, quick steps, and with his head well forward set the pace as we made for the first lot of wires. Have you ever been in someone's company and felt absolutely safe from all harm? That feeling came over me as I walked with these men of staid nature and vast experience. Some of Oliver's conversation with Mr. Carter will stick for ever in my memory, also their mannerisms and parochial outlook. This was the late twenties and early thirties. Millions were unemployed and as Oliver told his tales without thought of the depression he always ended with, 'That's the truth, the certain truth and the truth needs no study.' As we climbed a Cotswold stone wall he'd say, 'Jack be nimble, Jack be quick, Jack jumped over the candlestick.'

Mr. Carter told me of his father who was never tired. He just wouldn't be tired, he said. They talked of births and deaths in the village. Mr. Carter mentioned that another Bradfield had been born and Oliver said, 'Oi, they carries these parcels about so long then they drops um.' Mr. Carter added, 'I heard she was in the Chairoplanes at Evesham Mop last week.' Then he continued more seriously to talk of the text at chapel the last Sunday. 'I suppose, Oliver, that we're both on trespass down here. We're only promised three-score years and ten.' But to me that seemed a long way off, for as George Borrow's Blind Gypsy said, 'There's night and day, brother, both sweet things ... there's likewise a wind on the heath. Life is very sweet, brother.'

Here and there a snared rabbit could be seen in the light of the lamp, sometimes sitting quite still, to be quickly killed by Oliver or Mr. Carter dislocating its neck, the next perhaps already dead, the sudden stop as its head went in the snare breaking the neck at once. You see, I am not going to be foolish and say it's always possible to kill a rabbit painlessly. But one of two things happens with rabbit wiring—the rabbit is killed instantly or it squats still until it's picked up and killed. Scientists told us in 1954 that death from myxomatosis was painless. I would say that nothing like this disease has ever hit wild life in Britain in the remembrance of man. The roads covered with their stinking bodies, their heads swollen to twice their normal size, blinded and oozing pus. All this was disgusting to witness; I killed scores. I'm glad that Oliver and Mr. Carter never lived to see myxomatosis.

Mr. Carter kept about six ferrets in some rabbit hutches near the bull-pen. He usually had one or two fitchers (black and white ones). On Saturday afternoons we worked some of the holts, usually with a liner ferret (one with a collar on attached to a strong string line). The rabbits would sometimes bolt when Mr. Carter or Oliver shot them but often would get into a dead end and several would be spouted up there. Mr. Carter's Italian greyhound had a good nose and ear on these occasions, and we would lie on the ground with our ears close to the grass and listen to noises like thunder as the ferrets chased the rabbits into these spouts, all the time the line on the ferret jumping through Mr. Carter's fingers as the ferret leaped after its prey. When all this was over and the line was tight, we either followed the line by digging with a graft or dug where the dogs scratched and struck the hole. Sometimes the ferret, after killing a rabbit, would lie up and sleep with a full stomach. Oliver, if we had a hold-up of this sort, paunched a rabbit and blew the fumes from the freshly paunched rabbit down the hole to entice the ferret out.

Dad and my Cousin Tom were ferreting one cold January day about 1928 on Furse Hill. It was towards four o'clock and they had had a goodish day when they put the ferret in a holt towards the Horse Camps. The hole here ran to a depth of five feet into limestone, fox earthy soil and then pure sand. It was tedious following the line as the ferret had gone some distance and the soil fell back in behind. My Cousin Tom, kneeling down pulling the soil back to clear the hole, found the line and pulled one rabbit out and then the ferret. 'Uncle,' he said to Dad, 'there is something here shaped like a basin.' He pulled it out and it was a human skull, its teeth shining like pearls. They put it back, Dad saying, 'Let the poor chap rest,' and went home after filling in the hole. Next morning I went up and found a few perfect teeth on top of the ground and also some horses' teeth. A neighbouring landowner told this story to an archaeological society which arranged to have a dig. Dad said that my cousin Tom would show them just where to dig. Joe Baker said that there was no need and he went up with his divining apparatus and wasted a day for himself and the society, as they dug in various places where Joe said it was and found nothing. A pity really. It might have revealed a bit of local history.

CHAPTER THIRTEEN

TOM WHEATCROFT AND JOB BARLEY

IN THE 1920s and years after, if anyone had asked me who of all the men in the land I admired most of all my reply would have been (apart from Dad, of course), 'The shepherd and Tom Wheatcroft.'

Tom was one of a large family; he lost his father when he was very young and knew from bitter experience as a lad what it meant to go hungry. When I first knew him he was a fine, upstanding middle-aged man, a waggoner for Wilfred Little-wood. His team was the best in the village. He broke in shire colts, worked them until they were five years old, and they were then sold for working in the towns. Later he was stockman for David Meadows at Whitelands, and had a Scotch collie named Daffy which he thought the world of. It was when he came as stockman at our place that I really got to know him.

For a year or two I was a sort of understudy to him but almost lived with him at work during school holidays. We were rearing calves and not milking when Tom came. After he had suckled the calves and fed and watered the cows and store cattle in winter, there were about forty strong store cattle wintering on the top of Bredon and after ten o'clock bait I went up there with him to help him 'fother' them, as he said. We kept Turpin, a dependable horse, up there for the winter, a set of fillers gears and a muck-cart to cart the hay to the forty stores, which were also having cake ready for Gloucester market about April time. We called at Paris, the little hamlet two grounds away from our village, and Tom popped in a little cottage there to see if his aged mother was all right. The tales he told me on the journeys! 'You can't remember Bishampton Harold, that entire (stallion) Wilfred Littlewood used on his mares?' 'No, I can't, Tom,' I replied. 'Well, if you can't remember him, and mind ya, he was

Villagers at the fifteenth-century cross, c. 1880

Ashton Village Club, with band, *c.* 1908

Ashton Club Day, *c.* 1914

William Hooper, standing, landlord of the Plough
and Harrow, *c.* 1920

Grafton mower, reaper and digger, Teddy Vale,
outside his cottage in the late 1920s

Boys of Ashton-under-Hill, c. 1912

Haymaking in the late nineteenth century

Ricks on staddle stones at Crump's rickyard

the finest hoss that ever travelled these parts, you'll remember some of the colts he got.' He then rolled off a list of horses' names, some I knew and some I didn't—Sharper, Violet, Boxer, Bonnie, Prince, Slarrops. 'When your Dad sends us to Beckford sale in the Spring, I expect he'll send a few stores there. We'll have a look at the Winchcombe Hoss. I have heard as he is related to Bishampton Harold. If he's as fine a seventeen hands as *he* was he will do. Still, Fred,' Tom continued, 'yer Dad and Master Carter don't breed any colts now since they bought that bunch of yearlings from Gloucester. Except, of course, the one we had for nothing when that young mare Pleasant got out to the Captain's hoss and bred young Prince.'

We walked and talked our way to Great Hill Barn, where a light powdering of snow had brought Turpin alongside the wall of the barn, Tom remarking, 'He knows where to get to be in the borough (shelter).' The forty heifers were standing ready for their hay and cake. 'Good job we ant got to start a fresh cut on the rick today. The thatch ud be cold to the fingers.' We harnessed Turpin in the cart and Tom sharpened the cutting knife with his whetstone or rubber, making a musical ring as it slid first one and then the other side of the cutting edge. Possibly some of the old full-time hay trussers could handle a hay knife better than Tom (they did nothing else), but as Tom drove the blade into the hay almost up to the handle with apparently little effort he soon had the first square kerf cut. He got back on to his ladder, struck his shuppick into the hay, and a square mattress of pressed hay fell from Tom's shuppick into the bed of the cart as Tom pitched it off the rick. I trampled it down firmer into the cart, and kerf after kerf soon made a cart-load for the hungry heifers. When the cattle had had enough hay drawn out into the Barn Hill, Tom gave them their allowance of cake in little half-barrels cut for the purpose. We came home a different way down the old waggon track. 'Master Blackwell have got a fresh lie-by,' Tom said as we passed a cottage down the village street. 'Yes, a housekeeper from Cheltenham.' Tom cleared his throat and thinking it wiser to talk to me in riddles said, 'Oi I dare say if thur was a fire they ud both cum out of the same bedroom winda.' As we came to the Plough and Harrow Tom said, 'It's about five to one. I'm going to have half a pint of cider.' I walked the other few hundred yards alone, leaving Daffy lying outside the pub door. I thought that if ever a man earned half a pint Tom had. Doing more work that morning for about three and sixpence than plenty would do in a week.

Tom did a bit of pig castrating in his spare time, and was very proud of his bone-handled shut knife, once the property of Nailus, the Squire's shepherd.

His stories of happenings at Wilfred Littlewood's were told with relish. Wilfred used to go off and leave Tom in charge. 'Wilfred,' he said, 'bought this here tractor, a "Whiting Bull", and they started ploughing the big ground. The thing was always going wrong and I had to take my four hosses many a time to pull him out when he got stuck.' Tom said he started ploughing one side of the big ground with his four-horse team and 'Wilfred and our Joe started the other side with this very early type of tractor. I told um I'd plough um out of the ground and I did, addledum (Headland) and all. I tell ya summat else, Fred. Nowadays they'll plough and plough with these yer tractors, padding the ground until thur's no mould left and it'll take the steam tackle to move the soil.'

Apparently at Littlewood's cider was on tap all day and every day and Walt, who later became our carter, and Jack Jinks, George Jinks' brother, sheared the sheep in the home orchard. Wilfred Littlewood had some strongish Oxford Tegs (yearling sheep) and Walt and Jack had a fair drop of home-made cider as they sweated and struggled with the sheep in the hot June sunshine. They kept on late at night but the cider got the better of them and several sheep got away with half their fleeces on. Tom told me this, but it was not common knowledge; Walt and Jack were working before daylight the following morning finishing off those that had only had short back and sides. Wilfred Littlewood would have made a good farmer had he taken Tom's advice. Tom tried hard to keep things going but some of the other men took advantage of Wilfred's carelessness.

Just as I left school in 1931 Dad bought some stirky little heifers from up in Yorkshire for calf rearing. They were short-horns, and there were six of them to replace some of the old cows. Tom never liked them from the moment we put them in the straw-littered yard at the back of our house. As they were a bit on the poor side Tom reckoned that they had had more mealtimes than meals. Neither Tom nor I was looking forward to the 1st May, when they would go out to grass. 'They be as wild as park hares,' Tom said. 'We be in for some fun.' Turning-out time came and Tom's predictions were right. They did lie on Paris Hill for a couple of days but as Job Barley would have said, 'Next morning they was there missing.' It was a hot and sultry May and the heifers soon got as far as Elmley Castle deer park. Tom said they belonged there, being as wild as bucks. Fetching back stray cattle is known in this area as 'cattle bump-ing' and as a lad of sixteen there was nothing I enjoyed better than working with Tom. It took us one day to find them and when we did they just would not drive. We opened the gates, circled round them in a wide arc and they would stand facing us with their hind quarters in the gateway. Then with one mad rush they would get past us. The second day was no more successful and Dad and Mr. Carter kept asking us if we had got them back. As we sat on a knolp on the Round Hill and ate our dinner Tom was quite composed and told me of similar inci-dents. 'What's a-going to happen when they "calves down"?' Tom said. 'Somebody's going to get knocked ass over yud. Whatever yer Dad bought um for, I don't know.' After dinner the weather went a bit cooler and the six heifers, refusing to go through two open ten-feet gates, jumped the fences and got into Ashton Wood. Here they were away from the flies and as we drove them around in circles the time came round to suckle the calves at Stanley Farm, and avoiding the two gaffers we went on with this job.

Next day Tom and I went mangold hoeing, where he showed me how to flat hoe mangolds before they were chopped out. The ground was hard and bleached with fertiliser and what's more the heifers were in the wood. 'Dost know what I bin a-thinking,

Fred?' Tom asked. I replied, 'About those heifers, I suppose.'
'Oi, if we was to take old Granny and Peasbrook (two veteran
three-quartered cows which had gone dry and were putting a
bit of meat on ready for market as fat cows), if we took um up
to Kessa that adjoins the wood and put um through into the
wood, perhaps when it gets cold towards dusk them Yorkshire
girls ud come out with them.' It worked. We got them back.
They eventually calved down, all quiet except one dark red,
wide-horned one which knocked me over in the barn as I led her
calf and the calf bawled out. We called her Badger because of
her striped face, and she reared a number of calves, having four
of her own.

If anyone wanted a description of Tom Wheatcroft, I think it
would be fair to say he was a vet who had never been to university and had no letters. Badger lost condition after her fourth
calf and was tied up in the long shed, looking very sorry for
herself. She had developed a cough, was scouring badly, and
refusing the most tempting food Tom offered her. The official
vet arrived, an Irishman who was very down to earth. He examined the cow which was making a roaring noise as she
breathed. Dad came along and said to Mr. Macquire that he
wondered if a piece of mangold had got stuck in her gullet.
Tom spoke up, 'No Master, if it was that her ud be swelled up
round the brisket.' Mr. Macquire jumped off his feet, put his
hand on Tom's shoulder and said, 'You have a good man here,
Mr. Archer. He's quite right. Do you know, I know of men who
have taken their degree at Edinburgh University who would not
have noticed that? It's T.B. Send for the knacker.'

When Tom worked on David Meadows's farm at Whitelands,
Job (or Joby) Barley was his ploughboy. At haymaking it was
Joby's job to take the full loads of hay from the meadows down
by the railway up to the farm with three horses and take back
the empty waggons. Joby came down with an empty waggon
one day into the New Piece where the pitchers and loaders were
working. 'I say, you blokes wants to mind what you be a-talking
about down yer. The Gaffer has got his field-glasses on up at
the bedroom window and he can hear every word. Another

thing, have any of you seen a shovel cos thur's one in the barn missing?' Young Joby was described by Tom as a gallus young mortal, and during the haymaking failed to come to work one day just when the hay in Eight Lands was as sweet as a nut and, as Tom said, in good order. Mr. Meadows in the stable the next morning said, 'Where were you yesterday, Joby? You weren't ill or anything?' 'No, Gaffer,' said Joby, 'I stopped at home and went to Brum.' Only he could have thought of that.

Now Tom and Joby liked to have a day at Stratford Mop or Bull Roast but this particular year they took Jim Bradfield, David Meadow's carter, with them. Stopping for that extra half-pint, they all three missed the train home and started walking the twenty miles back in the early hours of the Sunday morning. Finding an open cart shed with some hay at Abbots Salford they dossed down for the rest of the night. When they continued their journey on Sunday morning and were coming down Greenhill into Evesham, Joby made the classic remark, 'Where do you think about going to next year?' Tom and Jim arrived home for dinner and both had tongue pie from their wives. Tom told me after many years, 'We both deserved it leaving a wife and young uns at home.'

David Meadows was about the first to put pneumatic tyres on his carts, and seeing Joby with a flat tyre one day said, 'That tyre's flat. Put some wind in it.' 'Oi,' said Joby, 'but it's only just in that one place where he touches the ground.'

Joby carried a watch with him at work but couldn't tell the time. If you asked him the time he'd say, 'It must be pretty near dinner-time. Any road, that train's gone.' He told me one day that there was an extra train run in the morning 'full a' them thur expectors'. David Meadows knew Joby's capabilities and asked him one day as he was putting the dray harness on Polly, the nag, what time he expected to be back from Evesham market. 'That all depends on what time I starts,' Job said, weighing his words very carefully as he spoke.

I walked many miles with Tom taking heifers to local markets and when Dad brought them in unsold we often came home in the dark. Tom had been used to walking all his life and he told me that as a young married man before the 1914 war he often walked the six miles to Evesham on Saturday nights but took a short cut back by the Saltway Barn. He took his frail and in those days before refrigeration he said you could get a frail full of good meat for a shilling and they would almost throw it at you in the butchers' shops on a Saturday night. He lived well for a working man and said he was never any better off than before 1914 on fifteen shillings per week. During the last war he kept a pig in a sty at the back of his thatched house and fed it well to about sixteen score.

I remember his wife suggesting they start the hams in the spring of the year and Tom said, 'Leave them till I got some hard work to do, haymaking and harvesting.' At these times he would bring a good thick rasher and fry it on a stick over a wood fire. Catching the gravy on a piece of bread, he would say, 'Now then, Frederick, let's get that hay into one yup.' He taught me how to pitch and as I grew up and he got a bit past it I kept up with him, but I doubt if I could have done so when he was in his prime. He told me of Alf Taylor at Meadows's place pitching hay with David Meadows one Saturday afternoon when the weather looked threatening. 'Hold tight!' David kept on shouting as he urged the horses to move the waggon from one hay cock to another. Alf was determined to keep up with Mr. Meadows and was leaving a lot of rakings behind. Mr. Meadows, noticing this, said, 'Dall it, Taylor, let's have a part on it this time.' But I'd put Tom and Walt, our carter, when they were in their forties, against any hay pitchers I've seen. If Walt hadn't got a good pitchful he'd say, 'Yur's a bit about as big as a crow's nest. You better have this under yer fit.' The older workers always reckoned that if a pitcher 'grounded a shuppick' he had to treat his mate to a pint. ('Grounding a shuppick' meant allowing the tip of the pitchfork shaft to touch the ground when the worker was lifting a forkful of hay.) Now Tom was not as critical of 'fother' as the shepherd. His favourite saying about hay which was not quite up to standard was, 'I'll bet next winter them store cattle'll sooner yutt this than fore-fit or a snowball.' During the meat rationing Tom was not very pleased with the quality of the meat supplied by his butcher and said to him one Saturday, 'We had a bit of the old yow last wick, a bit of the old tup the wick afore, let's have a bit of lamb this wick.'

Tom's gone. We shall never see his like again. I always liked to hear him call Mother and Dad, 'Mam' and 'Master'.

CHAPTER FOURTEEN

BLENHEIM AND LAUGHING TOM

No one knows exactly why he was called Blenheim. Blenheim
Orange is a very good apple, but I suspect he got his name from
that poem we all learnt at school, *The Battle of Blenheim*:

> 'It was on a summer evening
> Old Kaspar's work was done,
> And he before the cottage door
> Was sitting in the sun . . .'

Be that as it may, Blenheim was almost as much a part of
Ashton (or Ayshon, he called it) as the village cross.

He was employed as cowman for Squire Bosworth's cousin,
Laughing Tom's father, who farmed The Bullens, a farm partly
in the Vale but stretching up the side of Bredon as far as the
Nap. Let's think of him in summer-time when the bree flies
were worrying his cows. He passed our house four times a day
to and from the cow-ground. His panama hat, once the
property of Mr. George Price, the artist, fitted him like a ready-
made shirt. He shaved he said, 'once a wick whether I needs one
or no', so by the weekend he had a fair stubble of sandy grey.
His fawn corduroy trousers, well yorked up with straps below
the knees, were as clean as his job would allow, and his Oxford
shirts, sleeves rolled up to his elbows, showed a pair of strong
nut-brown arms. In one hand he carried 'an aish plant', which
helped to propel him along in an ungainly fashion. I imagine
that what he called his 'gammy leg' was either arthritic or the
result of being kicked by some cow. He never told me, nor did
he complain about it.

Driving cows up the back lane and then up the village street
on a hot sultry day is a stop-and-go sort of job. The cows love

the shade of the overhanging bushes and trees up the side of the grass verges. They just won't walk on the road, preferring the grass which is softer for their feet, and getting the benefit of every bit of shade. A large elder, or 'ellun', as Blenheim called it, covered in white bloom and giving off a rather sickly scent, stood in the hedgerow overhanging the ditch and the grass verge where Blenheim's cows walked nose to tail in a worn path they had made in the grass. The herd of about twenty cows included a cross-bred Jersey called Brindy. Brindy was usually behind, old, artful and a bit tender on her feet. The cows lingered under the elder, a few at a time. It was a safe retreat from the flies and the hot sun. But not for long. 'Come on now. We ant got all day. Heigh up.' This reminder from Blenheim sent them scurrying on, tails erect, to the next haven, a drooping ash where the lane joined the village street. Blenheim then was really hurrying to move them on from there, his voice getting a little louder and yet more impatient. Outside our garden wall where the grass verge is wider stands an old lilac with low drooping boughs, ideal for cows to duck under in order to remove the flies from their backs. Blenheim and the cows knew that this was a hindrance on their half-mile journey to the farm at the Bullens. Brindy just stood there enjoying the shade and several 'cup, cup, cups' from Blenheim failed to budge her. On one such day we were haymaking, building a rick in the nearby rickyard. I heard Blenheim use one of his classic utterances. 'Brindy, I'll strike thee like Moses smote the rock when he was with the children of Israyhell if thee dosn't move on.' Brindy was too artful and Blenheim was too lame for her to come within striking distance of the ash plant and with her tail swishing the flies as she emerged from the cool of the lilac to the hot afternoon sun she trotted up the road.

I passed him on my bike and he shouted, 'Frederick, hasn't thee got no oil?' I said, 'What for?' He said, 'Put some on them wheels. My eyes, don't they holler.'

Blenheim's association with Laughing Tom was more evident after Tom's father died and Laughing Tom went into a sort of semi-retirement, just keeping a few cows, making a bit of butter, a nice lot of Old English Game Fowl, Gleanys and a few pigs. The one cottage at the Bullens was midway between Blenheim's cottage and Tom's house. This was used for one purpose and one purpose only, storing cider. On wet days the two of them, both bachelors, could be found in there drinking out of a cider horn a drink made from the real cider apples put into fresh-emptied rum casks. 'Two pints a this, my byoy,' Tom would say, 'ull make you start talking about yer grandfayther.' They thrived on it and the fattest reastiest yellow bacon I've ever seen. No one quite knew whether Laughing Tom was obliged to work or not. It was come day, go day, God send Sunday.

I must explain how he came by his nickname. He laughed at everything. He and old Blenheim used to do a bit of pig killing. Tom was an expert. In fact, he could do anything with animals. He killed several pigs for me. He would arrive on the appointed morning with all his tools in a straw frail. He also brought his own blacksmith-made shuppick hooks and ropes. We won't go into details but with modern humane killers it was soon over. The interesting part and the part which required a lot of skill was the burning-off of the bristles. He placed the straw all over, even some in the mouth, and lit it from the tail end, moving it with his shuppick so that the skin wasn't burnt. The cleaning needed lots of hot followed by cold water and then the pig had to be hung from the ceiling on a strong hook in the back kitchen. 'Hasn't got any hooks, Master Frederick? No, I thought thee 'udnst so I a-brought mine. I can have 'um back tomorrow.' After it had been dressed there was a lot of speculation on how heavy the pig was. Tom had brought his steelyard weighers with him. Blenheim said, 'I reckon as he's about sixteen score.' Tom would start laughing. 'Whatever bist thee a-talking about, mon! I'll bet as 'er yunt above fifteen at the outside. What does thee say, Frederick?' I wasn't in a position to argue with men who had seen almost as many leap years as I had Christmas days. The steelyards showed he was fifteen and a half score and Tom laughed again. 'Now everything is fit to eat in the pig,' he said, 'bar the squeal. I'll cut him up tomorrow at two o'clock.'

This was a real pantomime. The pig was put once more on

the pig bench. I had a boy of about sixteen working for me and he helped with the lifting. 'Now the fust job for the butcher byoy is to cut his snout off.' He marked the place with his chopper. 'Now hit him thur, Roy. That's it.' And a while after Laughing Tom turned to me and said, 'How dost want him cut up, Fred?' 'Use your discretion,' I said. 'Discretion be darned,' he said, 'There's as many ways a cutting a pig up as there is pigs. Dost want much mate out on him or dost want it left on the flitch?' I said, 'Leave it on the flitch.' Then he stopped and told us a tale about one he killed for Harry Stallard. He was as thin as a hurdle and Harry wanted plenty of griskin and spare ribs taken out and, laughing enough to choke, Tom said, 'I'll be dalled if you couldn't see through the flitches. Talk about streaky bacon. It ut a-made hoss whips.'

He had a name for every bone he took out. The back bone he called his Lazarus. 'How about his Lazarus, Fred? Do you want him out clean or some mate left on him? If you leaves some mate on the bone you can have some chines. They allus keeps them for christenings.' I had only just got married and with a wicked look in his eye and a laugh he looked at, first my wife, then me and said, 'Any signs of a christening, Frederick?' 'Not this time, Tom,' I said. 'We won't have any chines.' Laughing Tom and Blenheim packed their tools and Tom's blue apron in the frail, I paid the few shillings and it was almost tea-time. We had had the history of pigs he'd killed, been told to salt bacon, and how he shot a boar pig in a barn with a .22 rifle after it had come for him open-mouthed.

Now in Tom's orchard grew almost every sort of apple, some pears and plums. Blenheim and Tom picked the fruit and despite persistent appeals by the local market Laughing Tom would not touch his plums or pears until they were dead ripe. The fruit has to be firm to travel to distant towns and must be picked on the firm side. 'They beunt fit for another wick,' Tom would tell Blenheim. 'It ud be murder to pick um.' So although his fruit was ideal for immediate use it would not travel. Blenheim agreed. 'What's the good a-picking pears till they be mella?'

Though Blenheim was getting worse on his legs, he did a bit of ditching for a local farmer. It was sad to see him pass our house, but he had a strong will and told me, 'I beunt a-gwain on the parish.' The war was on and some wit asked him if he had got his papers yet. 'Who was it who had rheumatic and bellyache in the fust war and got old Dr. Overthrow to get him out of the army and never voted for him at the 'lection?' This was humour at its best and true as well. I doubt if Blenheim could write his name but he had a good memory. I was tempted and fell into his snare when I asked him one day as he carried his spade past our house if he was off rabbiting. Of course he was on this ditching job. His reply was to the point. 'Some on us a-got other things in thur yuds besides rabbiting.' A few years before, I, as a boy, was playing round the buildings at the Bullens with a boy of my own age named Jim. We got up in the tallet where Blenheim kept the hay. Blenheim was in the stable below just as Jim came down the ladder. I lay still in the hay and heard Blenheim say, 'Who hasn't got up there? I reckon thee hasn't got a wench up in the tallet.' I climbed down the hay rack and got away unnoticed.

Blenheim died, the last of a family who served the village well.

After Blenheim's death one harvest we were short-handed and Laughing Tom came and helped me harvesting. He and Job Barley pitched the sheaves and Roy and I loaded the waggons, The oats were full of thistles off a field on the hill and Tom threw the sheaves at us two or three at once, laughing all the time, and our legs were full of thistles. I said to Roy, 'We mustn't say anything. He's come to oblige.' And as the horses moved from stook to stook another barrage came from Tom. But at the rick he worked as handily as ever I saw a man work, building it up using his fork left- or right-handed. His cow was ill at the time and he used to give her a pint of cider every morning. Among his many old-fashioned tools he possessed a propang, a hollow stick weighted at one end which we were glad to borrow if a cow got a mangel stuck in her gullet.

Laughing Tom's dead now. I'm really sorry.

CHAPTER FIFTEEN

DAD'S FARM SALES AND THE SALVATION ARMY

DAD AND MR. CARTER were always going to farm sales and Dad often brought something back for us. I remember once he brought a grand piano which took up half our drawing room. Before my time, in fact before Dad was married, he went to a sale on the corner of Cole Street, Evesham. I believe the vendor was a butcher who was going to Canada. This must have been about 1906 and he brought three things that day—an eight-bore wild duck gun with a long barrel which kicked like a donkey, a phonograph and three Evesham pot hampers filled with records, and a Bradbury motor-bike. I never saw another one with such a side-car. It must have weighed nearly half a ton. The motor-bike lay abandoned in the barn under the hay loader and as a small boy I sat on it and blew the rubber-bulbed horn. It had been pensioned off and Dad had bought himself a nice governess cart, a cob named Polly, a liver chestnut, and a set of brown harness. We often went to Evesham and Cheltenham in this and little boys stood outside the King's Head at Evesham eager to earn a penny for standing by our cob while we did the shopping. Mr. Carter had an iron-grey cob, very fast, and a governess cart. Like Polly it was a smart animal but difficult to catch and sometimes took nearly all the men to corner it up in Tan Flun opposite his house. While on the subject of horses, I shall never forget the Candlemas Fair at Evesham, when giant shires were put through their paces in High Street, from the market to Restalls and back, while horsey-looking men with long whips watched them carefully as they were trotted, then walked, then backed, and their mouths and feet examined. Dad said they had little men to run with the horses; it made the horses look bigger. They looked big to me and well got up, with straw and ribbons in their mane and tail and a nice white halter. Horse copers, these dealers were called. But back to the motor bike. It was neither coil ignition nor did it have a magneto. The accumulator had to be charged periodically and a spare one was carried on the pillion. About this time Dad and Mr. Carter were buying orchards of fruit in Oxfordshire, mostly Blenheims and Sourings and the large Bittersweet in demand for mincemeat making. The motor bike was used to get to and from Chalbury and Kidlington but alas! when the return journey was started in the evening it was quite common for both batteries to be flat and they brought the motor bike back in the guards van of the train to Evesham. Dad used to tell me of pushing it to start and how he fell off it one day on the Workman Bridge when the road was covered with ice. A little boy with good intentions came up to him and said, 'Hurt yerself, master?' 'Don't talk to me, my boy!' Dad said as he rubbed his bruised knees.

At this time Dad and Mr. Carter played in the Evesham Salvation Army Band. Dad played an instrument known as a bombardon, a kind of sousaphone, which one got into. Uncle Fred, a little man, played a G trombone almost as big as himself and used to tell the tale of marching down High Street in Evesham and the band, then about thirty strong, turned left down Bridge Street. The drummer, Wilson someone, was so wrapped up in beating the big drum which he could hardly see over that instead of turning left with the band he kept straight on, across the market place. My Uncle Fred, being an original member of the band, told me of the rough times they had at the Four Corners of Hell outside the American Tavern at open air meetings on Saturday nights. The Skeleton Army attacked with flour and eggs, spoiling their uniforms.

There is nothing new in having stunts to attract people to religious meetings. Tom of the Fens was a desperate character seventy years ago but his life became changed by the influence of the Salvation Army from being that of a hardened criminal who had done everything bar murder. He came to Evesham to give his life story in the Town Hall and it was arranged for him to march in front of the Evesham Salvation Army Band dressed in his prison clothes with broad arrows on, handcuffed to Dad who was dressed in policeman's uniform. It drew the crowds and it proved a very successful venture. Dad did tell me that as he went back to the Army hall in the Leys to change that night, he caught some boys up to some trick or other, gave chase, and although he was in police uniform one of them shouted, 'It's all right. It's Tom Archer.'

When General Booth came along our turnpike road on his way to Cheltenham he rode in one of the first motor cars to come that way and half the villagers of Ashton flocked to the Pike to see it pass. Silver bands of all kinds, including the village bands, had a great attraction years ago. I personally think that we have lost something by the falling-off in popularity of the military band. There is something about the wind instrument played correctly which encourages, stirs and is thought-provoking. People today have different views about fox-hunting, but doesn't the sound of the horn do something to you? Recently I heard an expert blow the hunting horn at a fête and he described what the different calls meant. He finished by playing *Gone to Ground*, the farewell played at the grave of a huntsman.

When I was a small boy, before we had the wireless, Dad's phonograph was a constant joy on Sunday afternoons. The reproduction would be described today as shocking, but it was great fun. The records, cylindrical in shape, were taken from their cardboard cases and slipped over the cylinder of the machine, which looked rather like a typewriter. The needle was a permanent fixture but I could never quite understand why Dad had to periodically pour hot candle wax around it. The metal horn was fixed tightly by a little newspaper folded around the metal tube it fitted over. The governers went round and round to keep the speed constant, which only happened by continually winding the key. We have had little groups on our lawn listening to Ben Davies, a noted tenor, but before every record a nasal voice announced, 'This is an Edison Bell Record.' Marches seemed favourites, for example *The Double Eagle Washington Post*. Then we had *Little Boy Blue*, which made me feel quite sad when I thought of the sheep in the meadow and cows in the corn and poor Little Boy Blue under the haystack fast asleep. Dad, who had as a single man been a Salvationist, had a record of the old General Booth talking about the plight of the people in the slums. I can hear it now as I cast my mind back. 'They are born, they live, they eat, they sleep, and they die, all in the same chamber.' It didn't convey much to me then, but his last words to his son were, 'Bramwell, do something. People need our help.'

The duck gun stood in the corner of our workshop near the bench and vice and Dad did use it on occasions. It being an eight-bore, the cartridges were expensive and it was much too long for me to handle. My first gun was a number three garden gun. My brother used the duck gun for pigeon shooting after he had cleaned the barrel, and I believe it had a range of approaching a hundred yards. It had a nice walnut stock with a pistol grip but like Dad's muzzle loader it's no longer with us.

The motor-bike went for scrap about 1928. I do wish we had kept it.

The phonograph—well, an inquisitive boy who is now writing these lines was longing to know what made it go. So with a screwdriver he took the motor to pieces, releasing the spring which fled off our court wall halfway across the yard.

Dad and Mr. Carter grew less keen on sales and too often when Dad came in to tea and I said, 'What have you brought back today?' he replied, 'Myself, my boy.' Of course they still went to the markets and when I helped to drive the cattle to Evesham, there was a wide strip of grass near Hinton Cross where the cattle grazed and we had our bait. Dad used to tell us to drive them quietly, not to rush. 'Let them graze. You got plenty of time.' Then Mr. Carter came in with his 'Swift' car, met us in the market, took us to Churckleys for cocoa and lardy cakes.

Later Dad had a Sunbeam tourer and I helped him fetch young calves from Gloucester market, in the back. We have brought back six at a time, me in the back, with calves tied to the hood, licking Dad's ears. Farming in those days was a precarious job. More money was made from rabbits than crops. But

Dad always said, 'If you keep rearing calves, they will grow into the money.' The price of a good calf then was five pounds. We sold a good bunch of stores every spring, and although there were seventeen men and boys to pay there were no big machinery bills to meet. Looking back, although labour was cheap, a bit more mechanisation would have paid.

CHAPTER SIXTEEN

VILLAGE CRICKET AND UMPIRES

OUR VILLAGE, being a relatively poor one, was later than some in playing organised cricket. There was no half-day holiday on Saturdays sixty years ago for land workers.

On the 28th January 1907, a meeting was held in the school. I have the minutes in front of me now. The Reverend Hornsby, the curate, was appointed captain and a set of rules was drawn up. The first six rules were quite ordinary and could have applied to any cricket club, but rule number seven was different. This rule stated that the committee reserved the right to dismiss any member for disorderly or bad conduct on the ground.

The vice-captain appointed was Mr. Arthur Jackson, a small farmer, whose holding was on the hill. The cricket ground belonged to Mr. Fred Beasley, a large farmer who let the ground to the club for one pound per year.

The first match was fixed against Norton and Lenchwick on the 1st May 1907. The pavilion in the Broadenham was an old railway carriage and things looked set for a good season. But at a general meeting held on the 15th August 1907, about six months after the formation of the club, a letter was read by the secretary from Mr. Fred Beasley giving notice to the club that he refused to let one of the members, namely Arthur Jackson, play in any other match that season on his ground owing to some grievance between themselves. The trouble was that Mr. Jackson's cattle had broken through the fence into Mr. Beasley's mowing grass and the two men had fallen out. The chairman explained that it was the duty of the members to decide whether Mr. Jackson had broken any of the club's rules and what steps they should take in the matter. The meeting came to a most unusual decision. They decided by a majority of seven votes that Arthur Jackson had broken rule number seven and that he was barred from playing again that season. Mr. Fred Beasley then went on renting the ground to the club. A stormy year for the first year of a village team! How Arthur Jackson broke rule number seven by disorderly conduct on the field, when what really happened was that he had had words with Fred Beasley over his cattle breaking through into some mowing grass a mile away from the cricket pitch, no one can explain.

Next year, Arthur Jackson, who had been dismissed from the Ashton Cricket Club, started with Alf Pickford, the younger Alf Pickford and a few more who took Jackson's part, in what became known as the United Cricket Club. The new club played in a field of Alf Pickford's known as the New Piece. These two teams ran 'at loggeryuds', as Charlie Bradfield said, for three years. When a meeting was held in the school on the 10th May 1910, Mr. James Longfield was in the chair. He had recently come to live in the village and said the purpose of the meeting was to try and bring the two committees together and all would work together as one club. After a lengthy discussion the United Club agreed to throw in their lot with the Ashton club, having representatives of both clubs on the committee.

Young Alf Pickford objected to serving on the committee and his father proposed, and it was carried, that he should be fined one guinea. It was decided that night that if any disputes arose in the club between members at the committee meeting or in any other way all disputes should be settled by the president and chairman, Mr. James Longland. Mr. Longland agreed to give a bat to the player with the best average. After this troublesome start the club went from strength to strength and reached its heyday in the twenties when Mr. Edgar Longland, the son of the president, was captain and with the aid of an excellent groundsman produced a wicket near the station which was the talk of the district. High scores were commonplace; the outfield was as good as the square. Old-time umpires were a race apart and Lofty Summers was no exception. Ashton were playing Dumbleton and the last pair were batting for the visitors when Harry Shakespeare, Ashton's fast bowler, bowled a yorker. The Dumbleton batsman, playing with his bat and pad close to-

gether, edged the ball with his bat on to his pad. Lofty shouted,
'Out!' 'How can he be out?' the Ashton captain said. 'There's
been no appeal and he played the ball with his bat.' Lofty was
unmoved. 'The ball hit him on the leg and anyroad I wants my
tay and he's out.' Whether this affected the result of the match,
I can't say, but it was an unusual decision. A visiting team from
the other side of the hill were playing on our home ground and
their umpire with his white smock and his pipe going appeared
to be watching the game but one appeal brought the reply, 'Not
out, but if it occurs again it will be, to an appeal for l.b.w.'

Edgar Longland, apart from being a keen cricketer and a
good sport (he encouraged us boys), was a bit of a wag and he
wanted a blacksmith to work on his farm to shoe and do repairs.
He put an advertisement in the local paper for a blacksmith,
preferably one who could play cricket. Whether Caleb Batchelor
had ever handled a cricket bat before is a thing no one will ever
know, but he was a useful blacksmith and turned out for the
team on the Saturday. I shall never forget him. He wore white
flannels but with broad braces and a leather belt with a huge
brass buckle. His arms were like legs of mutton, well tattooed,
and as he waddled out to bat at about number eight the locals
were wondering how he would shape. I think the team was
Alcester and Ragley, one of the best teams we played. Caleb took
centre for the first ball from their fast bowler. He ran up the
pitch, turned a well-pitched ball on the off into a full toss and
sent it as if he was hitting the anvil to the square leg boundary.
His sledge-hammer strokes produced the runs and the better the
ball, the harder he thumped it. Straight drives went to long on
and agricultural strokes to leg. After he had made fifty he was
caught out on the square leg boundary, but he had played himself into the team. I suppose that after a day swinging a sledge-
hammer this was child's play to Caleb. The day he made
history in our village was when he hit a six over the scoring hut;
it landed at Gloucester twenty miles away. You see the ball
landed in an open railway truck as a goods train passed through
the station and was found when the train stopped at Gloucester.

Besides the sloggers we had also some classical batsmen.

Gordon Johnson, who got his county cap for Gloucestershire, was as fast a bowler as we had, an excellent slip fielder and a batsman who played all the strokes in the book. The week after he gained his county cap he turned out for the village team. He batted in that honoured place, first wicket down, and as he came down our pavilion steps, immaculate in his Gloucestershire cap, we schoolboys sitting on the grass by the red withy tree thought we were in for a treat. He walked out to his crease and one or two gentlemen with cigars clapped him as he took middle and leg. The first ball well on the leg side he padded up to in the orthodox country style. The umpire at the other end sitting on his shooting stick, after an appeal by the bowler, raised the dreaded finger and Gordon Johnson was on his way back to the pavilion. Old Charlie Bradfield said, 'Oi, Gordon used a word when he went up them pervilion steps as yunt in the prayer book. Looks bad, ya know, when he had bin a-playing for the county. But I'll tell tha what it is, Fred, thee never wants to let that ball hit yer pads when old so-and-so's a-empiring. You'll be out else.'

Around the scoring hut a group of youths lazed on the grass and put the numbers of every ten runs that were scored or when a wicket fell. If someone was out for a duck, or a quack, a nought was not put up but a rather nicely white-painted duck on the metal square was pegged on the board.

Howard Walsey was a regular umpire and had a little wire-haired fox terrier named Nip. Nip lay on the grass by the scoring hut while Howard was busy umpiring. The lads, who will remain nameless, tied a tin-square duck on Nip's collar, and after Nip had circled the boundary he went to his master at the wicket. By this time the culprits had fled into Catherine's Meadow as Howard ran, waving his shooting stick and threatening the youths who had run away.

Edgar Longland was ever ready to put on stunts to raise money for the club and charity. One evening a match was staged in which the men, dressed as women, batted left-handed with withy sticks, and bowled and fielded left-handed, and the women's team were dressed in flannels. I picture now Fred

Hinton, our wicket-keeper, dressed in a long red velvet dress with lace accessories and an enormous black straw hat trimmed with cherries. Short skirts were really in fashion and some of the men had difficulty in keeping their stockings up. As the box went round for the Red Cross the very ordinary comment would be that a good time was had by all. Percy Bostock from Beckford played in his white flannels, commenting that he wasn't going to make a fool of himself. The cricket prospered until the 1939 war and now is as popular as ever. But Caleb Batchelor's sledge-hammer strokes and his leg-of-mutton arms are just a memory.

CHAPTER SEVENTEEN

AUNTIE PHOEBE'S POP; HAYMAKING

THE NUMBER of people who quenched their thirst with a pint-and-a-half bottle of Auntie Phoebe's pop for twopence will never be known. It was good heady stuff made from some ancient recipe and was at its best when it was about a week old. We thrived on it in the June hayfields. Auntie Phoebe didn't charge any deposit on the bottles but most people took them back. The sorts and shapes of her bottles varied from square-shaped coffee-essence bottles to long wine bottles which Tom Wheatcroft kept because they had a long neck for drenching cows. Auntie Phoebe kept a little sweet shop in the front room of her thatched cottage but pop was her best-seller during the summer. She brewed this in a copper furnace and when she had bottled it all the corks, which had a slit across the top, were tied in with pudding string. If we just wanted a glass this was a penny. It was stone cold and refreshing. Apart from pop, Auntie Phoebe made and sold raspberry vinegar and home-made mushroom ketchup. The big horse mushrooms for this were gathered by Oliver, our rough carpenter, who lodged at Auntie's.

Oliver took a bottle of pop with him to work in the summer and for weeks on end kept off the cider. You see, Oliver never dabbled in anything and when he had what he called a session, it was serious. There was a special quart cup kept for him at the pub. A pint would have been an insult to him and for a few days he would be backwards and forwards past our house and once more he would have broken his resolution not to have another spot of cider. He was a man who, I firmly believe, had a heart of gold, but when he returned to work after a few days of heavy drinking Tom Wheatcroft described him as 'conterairy'. Oliver often loaded the waggons and if every pitchforkful of hay wasn't placed on the waggon by the pitchers exactly where Oliver wanted it he complained. This soon wore off and Oliver was back to his usual genial mood.

Tom and Walt were our best hay pitchers and Oliver and Shepherd Corbisley were a well-matched pair loading the waggons. But when the shepherd was wanted as rick builder a blue-eyed, fair-haired Welshman helped Oliver to build the loads. He, like so many of his day, had arrived by road with his little bundle and stayed in the harness room next to the nag stable where there was a fireplace; he was there for years. We called him Taffy, of course. He was one of the few who could be termed as roadsters that I was a bit afraid of. I remember he threatened to put the prongs of a hay fork through a youth of my age on the farm. But he amused us with some of his tales of farming on the Welsh hills. If no one answered him he would be upset and say, 'Did ya hear what I do say, mun?' Tales of sheep stealing were amusing at lunch-times, but when he told us how several of his companions murdered the shepherd on the Black Mountains we were careful to agree with him and not to argue. Walt was taken ill one summer and Taffy took over the cartering, being quite handy with horses. Several weeks before mowing started he chain harrowed and rolled the Dewnests, three meadows near to Carrants Brook. The day he finished harrowing it was about twelve o'clock and he, like the rest of the carters, worked until three o'clock. He had long gears or traces on his two horses and had no filler's tack or cart saddle and he was a mile from the stable. He needed a cart saddle to start rolling. Taffy hooked his two horses abreast to the back of the roll frame and carried the shafts himself until knocking-off time, the horses pulling the roll over the meadow backwards. A strong man, who was possibly not unlike the characters George Borrow met that Saturday night on Ruabon Mountain.

Haymaking, as I like to recall it, was at Great Hill on Bredon when the sainfoin rick was built. Sainfoin is a Cotswold clover rather similar to lucerne but with a red flower which flowers early. This twenty-five-ton rick was built in the same place every year handy to the barn on a straw staddle or foundation.

Walt mowed the Peewit Hill and as the sainfoin wilted I had old Captain in a primitive swathe turner and turned the swathes. Captain only had one speed—dead slow; and Tom Wheatcroft jokingly got behind a larch tree up there and I asked him what he was doing. 'Just a-seeing if thee wast a-moving.' The smell of the new-mown sainfoin, the circling peewits, the larks ascending, and summer-time was on Bredon. When Frank and I horse-raked the made hay into walleys I was allowed Flower and he the more agile Pleasant. We had to get the rows of hay in the walleys fairly straight because, if it worked, the Greens' hay loader was used to pick up the hay. This was hitched to the back of the waggon and two younger men loaded it. With three horses snatching at the traces, the loaders had to be sure-footed when Walt and I or Frank led the team, straddling the walleys or rows of hay which we had raked up before. When the loaders got 'mowed up' or had too much hay coming up into the waggon they shouted 'Whoa'. It was then difficult to start a nearly loaded waggon with this loader behind without the horses snatching. 'Hold tight,' shouted Walt. I held Turpin, the foremost, under his chin, tightening the bit in his mouth from both sides of his 'mullin' or bridle acting like the choke chain on a dog. If, by Turpin snatching, one of our loaders had been pitched off, Dad or Mr. Carter might have sent me scaring birds off the peas, and I wanted to be among the hay. Dinner-time in the hayfield miles from anywhere, the horses pulling their well deserved meal from the back of a loaded waggon, and then a half-mile trek with them to the stone trough on Furze Hill to water them can never be erased from the memory.

Then as about fourteen men and boys sat down in the shade of the beech trees and listened to the wisdom of these older men, who were the salt of the earth, Frank and Geoff and I, all boys, just drank in the stories of poaching from Oliver and of hay as it should be made, when more work was put into it, from the shepherd. Mr. Carter told us of harvesting all day with two hooks and how his small brother forgot to bring him his dinner and he worked until dark 'not having bit nor spot all day'. Then he told us about Joseph Arch speaking to them from a farm waggon about joining the Workers' Union. 'It was old Lloyd George who give us the pension,' the old shepherd said. 'See what they have done to Elliot,' (then Minister of Agriculture) he went on. 'Throwed eggs and tomaters at him and he'll get wo'se than that 'it.'

My small tin of sardines for dinner nearly brought tears to my eyes when the key broke. Dear old Uncle George opened them with his pocket knife. Uncle George was called Uncle by everyone and although he was not the handiest man in the hay-field he was as straight as a die. Besides Auntie Phoebe's pop, Uncle had a flask of tea. This was the first flask I saw and he poured the first cupful into *The Daily Chronicle* of the day before, for his liver and white spaniel, Tiny, to drink with a little condensed milk. If Dad and Mr. Carter were there (they usually were) we had just the hour for dinner. When Uncle was in charge he'd get up at two o'clock, dead on time, and pulling out his watch, came out with his usual, 'I do believe if I didn't make a move you jumping byoys 'd stop here all day.' Frank and I had cheap watches and would say, 'It wants another two minutes to two.' Uncle, whose watch could be relied on like Big Ben, said, 'Mine was right by Beach's hooter at eight o'clock this morning and I'll tell ya what it is, you can't do too much for a good master.' 'Poor old Uncle's got past it,' one of us would say. 'Yes, and you chaps a fellas ant got to it yet.' We teased him and it got back but the beauty of it was that he bore no malice. He would have given us his last drop of pop.

After dinner the shepherd, Dad and Tom Wheatcroft started making the staddle or rick bottom from some straw Walt had brought up and the waggons were unloaded, first by hand, until the rick reached about eight feet high. Then came the moment everyone had been expecting—the raising of the monkey pole. These poles were in two sections, jointed like a fishing rod and were used to elevate the hay from the waggon on to the rick. To raise the pole upright, half a load of hay was left on the waggon and the pole jointed together lifted on the waggon, the top at an angle over the shaft horse's head and the butt end or bottom of the pole secured by two iron spikes driven through two rings into the ground. Dad stood on the waggon and as Walt backed the filler or shaft horse the pole became more upright. Fixed to the top of the pole on a swivel were four guy ropes (sometimes wires). A man held each one of these as the pole became almost vertical. This was the point of no return. Dad gave out his orders quietly, 'Hang on to yours, Tom. Let yours go a bit, George. Come round a bit, Taffy,' and so on. Oliver then drove long iron spikes into the ground with a sledge-hammer. These had T pieces on the top; guy ropes were tied to the stakes and we breathed again. A steady shaft horse was vital. It was Captain again. A pulley wheel at the foot of the pole was for a rope to be threaded through which ran alongside the rick and passed between the load and the rick. The rope from there was taken up the side of the pole around another pulley on the crane-like jib. From there it was led to another pulley on the end of the jib and fastened to two enormous forks like grappling irons, sharp, three-pronged and heavy. Captain was hitched to the end of the rope on the ground alongside the rick and when the forks or grabs were shoved into the hay on the waggon a good forkful was raised off the waggon as Captain moved a few yards forward. The jib by a slight angle on the pole swung across and over the rick and the unloader on the waggon pulled a trip cord and the hay fell in a heap in the rick. Captain then had to be backed to give enough slack rope for the forks to be again pushed in to the hay on the waggon. As I led Captain to and fro, Jack Bradfield unloaded, and by keeping my eyes open I enabled things to work like clockwork. But Captain had a very hard mouth and he took some backing. He would see-saw at his bit and if Walt was unloading and getting a bit impatient, he'd shout, 'Let's have a bit more pudding. This don't half give my arms summat.'

'How's that corner of the rick, Fred?' Tom Wheatcroft, who was building it, would shout. 'Put it out about a foot,' I'd say, if I thought he was drawing it in, but he came off the rick every load he had a look around to see if we were going on all right.

When Tom went to suckle the calves, milk the house cow and

feed the weaned calves at four o'clock, the shepherd took over
the building, but when I got to be about twelve years old Dad
would send me down off the hill to suckle the calves because
Tom couldn't be spared. I got the milking cows in out of Tun
Flun, tied them up in the long shed and let the calves out of
their pens to suck them. Old Grannie was the house cow and it
was like getting blood out of a stone to milk her. Her own calf
had what was left and as Tom didn't want to make a pig of
himself he gave me instructions to 'Mind and get a bucketful
out of old Grannie afore you let that calf suck.' I could just
about handle her great teats in my small hands and as I sat on
that greasy old three-legged stool with my cap on back to front
I wrested half a bucketful from Grannie. She was unwilling to
let it down; she wanted to keep it for her calf. When I got back
to the hayfield the rick was three parts built and Dad and Mr.
Carter had been looking at some hay Walt had cut two days
before behind Grafton Firs. Mr. Carter's crystal set predicted
rain and Dad said, 'We'll turn it again and pick it up before
night and finish the rick.' The shepherd said, 'It's never fit in
this wide world. You'll have it fire as safe as eggs. Rain! It
won't rain, the wind w'ere tis.' It was picked up a bit green, or
'gay' as Tom said. It didn't fire, but the top of the rick got warm
and was a brown colour and smelt of tobacco when Tom cut it
in the winter for his store cattle. The shepherd had some of the
better sainfoin out of the bottom for his ewes. Even that wasn't
just right. The horse rakes had knocked all the leaf off it. 'No
herbage,' he said. He lived to see some cut and made with the
tractor but told me, 'Them ship won't yut it; it stinks o'
paraffin.'

We had to turn an oatrick once because it got hot. Tom had
told us to wait, but we put it together. The heat was sore on the
feet as we turned the sheaves and Tom told the old shepherd we
had 'lost a gold watch in the rick and was trying to find him'.

Haymaking memories are happy ones. Saturday night Dad
and Mr. Carter would get all the vehicles they could lay their
hands on and all went pitching and loading hay as Walt
brought them up to our rickyard. The first load drew up to the

rick, the next close behind, and I have seen eight or nine waggons loaded on Saturday nights with their middle well filled in
case of a wet weekend, the last waggon being almost in the road.
What a sight! And there was something to start with on
Monday morning, unloading, first, the borrowed waggons, then
our own five. The hay from the Dewnests and Thurness had to
be hauled over the station bridge and as I had the leading rein
on the foremost and Walt led the filler we cantered over the
bridge. The loads were well roped. I can picture the men of
yesterday roping loads, hitching the rope to the hooks on the
side of the waggon and coming out with showers of hay seeds
gone down under their shirts. There were the old panama hats,
the billycock hats, battered trilbies and cloth caps; the broad
braces of the men, whose noses dripped with sweat as they
worked to save a valuable winter feed. The wage was sevenpence
farthing an hour and ninepence an hour overtime.

Mr. Carter and Dad never advertised for labour. I'll tell you
why. They both knew what a good day's work was and working
with them got it from the men. I firmly believe that Mr. Carter
and Dad could give a lesson if they were with us in the relation-
ship between employer and employee. There were two masters
but they spoke as one and were more eager to encourage and
give praise where it was due than to criticise. Haymaking is still
an uncertain and hazardous job, but both master and man made
hay while the sun shone and took it a little steadier as the rain
took over, hoping that tomorrow the sun might be shining.

CHAPTER EIGHTEEN

THE PEA-PICKERS

DURING THE 1920s Mr. Carter and Dad grew a large acreage of peas. Varieties such as Early Bird were planted the first week in February if the ground was in the right condition. A succession of planting took place during the spring and summer, from the round-seeded Early Bird until the final plantings of Senator and Lincoln, which were planted on the flat top of Bredon. The late peas were planted there because they were less likely to get mildew. You see, the breeze which usually blows on the hill doesn't harbour mildew like the damper Vale with its autumn fogs.

The first pickings have been on the 31st May and the last on Armistice Day. The pea-pickers were a mixed lot indeed. They arrived in May, that is, the travelling type. Staff and Aggie were usually first and dossed down in the first pigsty next to the trap house. Some, like these two, had just enough money to tide them over until picking started. The casuals, or 'roadsters' we called them, were later reinforced with the Cheltenham Lower Dockham crowd, who left their houses and lived in 'bivvies' or tents of sacking under the hedges when all the buildings were full. We never knew their real names, but they may be divided into groups. First of all there were the ones named after the part of Britain where their original home was, for example, Staff (Staffordshire), Brummie (Birmingham), Cock (London), Manchester, Scottie, Devon, etc. The others had to have some means of being identified and so there were Joe, the Doings, Darkie, a Suffolk navvy who lived in the Cross Barn with Scottie, who had been first engineer on an ocean liner; and Mick and Jim, who lived in the granary with Cock and Brummie. Then there was a little man with rough whiskers and a rougher dog; and Little Titch, a friend of his, who cut his corns and changed his toe rags in front of the cart hovel; Sacko, his ginger wife, and a swarm of children. There was Annie Shaw from Lancashire, and Trotting Johnny who just trotted everywhere compared with Hopping Annie, a woman with a wooden leg and a filthy tongue. Little George lived at Great Hill Barn and came down on Saturday for his pay and shopping.

In those days all our cattle were at grass for the summer and the pickers took over. A motley crowd; bare-footed children—I remember one whose father was a widower left with a four-year-old boy, a sweet little chap. Our old Light Sussex cockerel used to chase him across the yard to our back door, where Mother used to dry his tears and give him a sweet. If his father was near and the little fellow didn't say 'Thank you' straight away, he'd say, 'Mind yer manners, my boy, in front of Godly folk and gentry.' The tragedy of all this to me was that lots of these roadsters had fought through the First World War and came to this precarious life. It was different with the Lower High Street lot from Cheltenham; they had homes of sorts to return to in the autumn. Tom Wheatcroft and I were horse-hoeing sprouts near the main road one day just as the hordes of broken men and women were on their way from Evesham to Cheltenham or Tewkesbury workhouse (or the 'Grubber' as he called it). I complained about some small thing and Tom said, 'Oi, the hardest work thur is, my boy, is to carry an empty belly along that turnpike road.'

The pickers were paid a shilling for forty pounds of peas, picked either into a pot bag or a pot hamper. Uncle George weighed the peas from a tripod, made from larch poles by Oliver, with a chain to suspend the spring balances. For every pot which weighed forty pounds the picker was given a cheque with 'H.C.' stamped on it, the initials of Harry Carter, Dad's partner. This worked very well, first of all because Uncle George had not any money on him and, secondly, the pickers could change their cheques when they needed the money by coming to our bay window overlooking the courtyard. We always knew whom to expect after tea. Staff and Aggie, Sacko and Manchester were regulars but Scottie and Darkie would not lower themselves to change their cheques every night; they came with the regular men for their wages on Friday nights.

We were always pleased to see Scottie arrive with his bag of few belongings about Whitsun. He kept himself spotlessly clean and after a few weeks' work bought himself a new hard cloth jacket and a pair of cord trousers. He blacked his boots and waxed his moustache on Sundays and walking up our village street, with little puffs of smoke coming from his pipeful of twist, he was the aristocrat of the pea-pickers. Summer nights as he and Darkie cooked their meals under the Warner's King apple tree at the back of the Cross Barn he kind of took the chair at a pea-pickers' parliament and he was a treat to listen to. I have heard of Keir Hardie; I imagine he may have been of the some kidney. Scottie detested strong drink but was a great gambler. Over his bed, which was partitioned off from the others in the barn by hurdles, he had written in copperplate writing, 'He who steals my purse steals trash.'

The Cheltenham crowd came for a good time, fresh air, a paid holiday, and an evening singsong at the pub. As our stock of shillings disappeared when cheques were changed, Dad sent me to John Merryweather at the pub with five pounds to ask him to give me a hundred shillings. A lot of these shillings had been spent by our pea-pickers and as old Charlie Bradfield said, 'Money is made round and it goes round.' In the cool bar on a summer evening as John counted out the hundred shillings, I read in letters of gold over the fireplace these words. 'As a bird is known by its note so is a man known by his conversation. Swearing strictly prohibited.' It struck me that a landlord of days before the pea-pickers came in their hundreds had put that up for local benefit. I mixed and mingled with people of all sorts. There were usually a hundred picking, and as the pickers asked Uncle George if their cousin or their uncle could pick peas, Uncle George said, 'You chaps be all aunts and uncles.' We seldom had any trouble on or off the field. I'd say they were a well-behaved lot. At the pub the singing was something out of this world as Caruso tried to outdo Paul Robeson and Gracie Fields competed with Melba. I listened from my bedroom window as *The Shade of the Old Apple Tree* changed to a piece by Gilbert and Sullivan. At closing time all were friendly and in our back yard I heard so often, 'Goodnight, Titch. God bless. We are pals, mind.' Then Joe, the Doings, would call him back and, with a hand on the shoulder, say, 'No offence to what I said. God bless, Titch.' This was repeated by the pickers as they returned to their separate stalls, a few at a time.

There was a great difference between the unfortunate roadster, with perhaps a wife and children, and the diddycoy. We would not employ them. Their horses and dogs were a nuisance, but one pea-picking they invaded the friendly atmosphere of our pub and started a pitched battle, throwing spittoons at each other all over some tart in a white silk dress who somehow joined them down Gypsies Lane. Shepherd Corbisley said to me, 'When them there spittoons started flying about I was in the bar and thought it best policy to go into old John's kitchen.'

I did say there was little trouble with the pea-pickers. That is true, but I vividly remember one July night at about eleven-thirty a squeal like murder coming from the lidded place at the end of the barn adjoining the duck-pen. Dad lit his candle and as Mother said, 'Do be careful, Tom,' he put an overcoat on top of his night-shirt, went downstairs in his slippers and found Joe, the Doings, fast asleep in Annie Shaw's manger. Joe had made a slight mistake where his bed was, and muddled with cider had laid in Annie's manger. Annie, a reputed spinster, took a dim view of this as she arrived home from the top pub and just squealed and squealed. A few words from Dad and all was quiet again as I leant out of my back bedroom window. Dad was quite unafraid of them and they treated him with respect. In fact, I don't ever remember him being afraid of anyone.

As the summer fled by and only the Lincolns on Bredon remained to be picked, the roadsters packed their bags, loaded their prams and went for another year. Scottie and Darkie were usually the last to leave and we were sorry to see them go. Scottie brought a little of the outside world into our village. But with Matthew Arnold we could say,

'He hearkens not! Light comer he is flown!
What matters it? next year he will return,
And we shall have him in the sweet spring days
With whitening hedges, and uncrumpling fern,
And blue-bells trembling by the forest-ways
And scent of hay new-mown.'

CHAPTER NINETEEN

ARMISTICE TEA AND THE MAGIC LANTERN

As THE dark winter evenings approached in our oil-lit village, the Armistice Tea in what was known as the Recreation Room or 'The Room' was looked forward to by everyone. The main object of the tea was to show a little appreciation of the Ashton men who had fought in the 1914 war. To quote the War Memorial, 'These men were a wall unto us both by night and by day'. The ones who failed to return were remembered that night also.

After the tea, the concert which followed was entirely impromptu. Reggie Nash had spent the afternoon carrying water from the standpipe by the village cross and waiting on the ladies who provided the tea. He lit the fire in the copper furnace and boiled the water for them, fetched the coal, trimmed the lamps and then, with the help of the porter from the station, fetched on a sack-cart the piano from the village school. The tea provided was the best of the year. Great hams and joints of beef were skilfully carved by Howard Cambridge, who had driven a model-T Ford in the Middle East. When Mr. Cambridge, Senior, was well enough, he took the chair at the concert. Failing this, Dad took his place. There was a little business to attend to before the entertainment began. Someone had to be appointed to care for the War Memorial garden for the next year and Mr. Penny was on this memorable occasion thanked by Dad, who was in the chair, for the way he had kept things tidy throughout the year just ended. This was agreed to by everyone except Joe Baker. These are his very words: 'When you be in the army they allus reckons to put the big soldiers at the back and the little chaps in front when drilling. Mr. Penny hasn't done that with his flowers. He has put little flowers at the back and these poor little fellows be trying their best to look over the heads of the big chaps at the front.' Mr. Penny proposed that Joe Baker be appointed to look after the Memorial for the next year, which was lightheartedly agreed to by everyone. In fact what happened was that they did the job together, being good gardeners and good friends.

The room was packed and the ex-servicemen, apart from having a free tea, were now handing the tobacco jar up and down the long trestle tables, filling their pipes full of tobacco and the room full of smoke. Others were content with a drag at a Woodbine, while Mr. Cambridge, Senior, when present, puffed at a Churchill-sized cigar. Mr. Robert Cambridge, a brother to Howard, opened the concert with a beautiful rendering of *The Londonderry Air* on his violin. He had difficulty in tuning it with the piano—the journey down the rough village street on the sack-cart had not done the piano any good. Miss Violet Baker, an excellent pianist, skilfully covered up some of the piano's faults by putting in twiddly bits. Edgar Macormick, a handsome man immaculately dressed in a blue suit with a chalk stripe and smoking a Sarony in a long cigarette holder, I imagine made the hearts of some of the young ladies of our village miss at least one beat. He didn't speak in our local brogue but had a pleasant public school accent without being affected. Working in insurance, he had not experienced clay on his boots since leaving Flanders with a commission. His song, *The Gay Drum Major*, appealed to us boys as we viewed the scene. The ladies were touched by 'Now we all can understand why the darlings love the band, especially the gay drum major.' The locals—sometimes their eyes were fixed on him, then they would wander to his cigarette and holder smouldering in the ashtray on top of the piano.

Henry Watson, a fruit and vegetable merchant, was originally a Black Country man but was well liked in our village. His activities ranged from choirmaster at the church to telling some very good stories of the Black Country where everything revolves around the pub and the 'cut' (canal). Year by year, he sang for his piece, *Trumpeter, what are you sounding now* in a very well-modulated voice, which almost dropped to a whisper

at the last sad verse. Howard Cambridge cracked jokes in between the songs and recited some of his own composition. As
Howard told us of the farmer's boy going for a job at Master
Brown's and Master Brown saying, 'Why are you leaving Master
Green's?', Shepherd Corbisley, sitting next to his wife by the
piano and smoking his clay pipe, exploded with bronchial
laughter before the end of the tale which he knew so well. 'I be
leaving Master Green's,' said the boy, 'on account a' the fittle.'
'Rubbish,' said Master Brown. 'I know Master Green would
give you ample to eat.' 'Oh, thur's plenty,' said the boy, 'but
fust the old cow died and we yut her; then the old sow died and
we yut her; then the old 'ooman died so I thought it was time to
leave.' Now Mrs. Collins from the shop sang 'I'm following in
Father's footsteps' in a Florrie Ford style. She had rhythm,
volume and a style which was in keeping with the spirit of the
evening. The recreation room was warming up. The stove was
red hot. Some of us went back-stage and helped to clear up
some of the jellies and trifle; others slipped out and produced
bottles of beer from under the steps which they drank under the
walnut tree in the orchard.

We listened intently to the conversations of the ex-soldiers,
tales of mud and rats. Then order was restored and the chairman asked Ernest, the thatcher, if he could think of a song. We
all knew what it would be. Ernest in his prime would rank with
the next as a fine countryman, a terrific worker and a man who
was afraid of no one. 'No,' he told me once, 'not if they was as
big as the side of a house.' He was a man to respect and agree
with for, though kind and gentle, when stirred he could fight
like a tiger. Besides hardships in the army, he had worked on
the Canadian railroads and just could not stand idlers. But back
to his song. He didn't need the piano, so Violet had a rest. He
stood against the trestle table dressed in his best navy blue suit
with his medals on his chest. He drew himself up to the six foot
two he was and then put the thumb of his right hand down
under his broad leather belt and moved the big brass buckle
slightly to one side. Clearing his throat, his eyes firmly fixed on
the rafters above him, he sang with feeling:

'If those lips could only speak
And those eyes could only see
From the beautiful picture
In the beautiful golden frame.'

This man had a personality which became infectious and as he
put the feeling and the tragedy into those old words, hearts were
stirred and memories revived of men the village people had
known and loved, but who had failed to return in 1918. Dad
now asked if we could all sing *Just a song at twilight when the
lights are low*—his favourite. The evening was going, slipping
away too fast for a schoolboy. This was the night we learned
more about people we had only seen at work in the fields,
hedging, gate-hanging, fruit picking and so on. These men were
completely natural tonight. Mr. Cambridge's gamekeeper and
shepherd sang *Tom Bowling*. A member of the church choir, he
was in good voice and he gave us *The Lincolnshire Poacher* for
good measure.

Walt, our carter, did need a lot of persuasion to do his bit.
The piano was not needed and Walt, with a certain lilt in his
voice, as if he were ploughing a lonely hillside, sang:

'I love the green fields
And I low the sunshine . . .'

All this could have been a bit of a muchness had it not been
for Howard.

Mr. Penny, a useful tenor, didn't trust the piano and brought
his tuning fork with him. He struck this on his knee and repeated, 'Doh, doh, doh,' until he was satisfied he had the right
note. 'Violet and I have only one line between us,' he said (one
copy of music). 'What are you doing on washing day, Mr.
Penny?' Howard said. 'What do you mean?' replied Mr. Penny.
'All your washing will be on one line,' was Howard's reply. Mr.
Penny ignored the little interruption and gave us *Santa Lucia*
with credit. More doh, doh, doh on the tuning fork and Mr.
Penny continued, asking the company to join in with *The*

March of the Cameron Men and *The Campbells are Coming*.
One of these, he told us, was the regimental march of the East
Lancashire Regiment, which brought forth 'Come on, you East
Lancs!' from Howard.

Joe Baker, the man of so many parts, gave an exhibition with
the bones and recited *The hen that laid astray*. Then his recita-
tion followed:

> 'I comes up from the country
> But I beunt so very green.'

'What about you, Shepherd?' Dad said, as Shepherd Corbisley was enjoying a clay pipe of Red Bell tobacco. 'I got it on
my chest tonight, Master,' he said. But with a prod from his
wife he sang a couple of songs between little choking coughs.

When the village baker, as good-humoured a man as ever
went to a party, sang his songs with a twinkle in his eye, we
were all silent in case we missed any words which he sang at a
rare speed:

> 'He bought her such a pretty wedding dress,
> 'Twas made by Mrs. Gottom.
> All embroidered round the bottom;
> Ting-a-ling-a-ling, Ting-a-ling-a-ling.'

He then sang *The Hawthorn Tree*. His voice on this occasion
was boyish and sweet. It went:

> 'I recollect when quite a boy
> Asking my Papa,
> "Where did I really come from?"
> "You'll have to ask Mama".'

The chorus was 'Underneath the shadow of the hawthorn tree'.

Mr. Stallard, the baker, was the salt of the earth, a man who
found time for everybody, even us lads, and our favourite song
of his was:

> 'John Brown he had a party
> On Tuesday of last week;

Tom Biggs was there as usual
With all his sauce and cheek.
He said, "You chaps, I just have pinched
A sovereign from a pal.
Shall we have smokes and drinks with it?"
I said, "Of course we shall."
We had whiskeys round and ninepenny smokes
And quite enjoyed the spree,
We laughed, we roared, we chuckled aloud with glee.
We screamed, we howled, we thought the joke was fine.
I didn't know till afterwards the quid was mine.'

John Harris, bass, painter and decorator, was all the time getting his strength up behind the stage, clearing up the ham and beef sandwiches which were left on the billiard table and swilling them down with cups of stewed black tea out of the two tea urns which stood by the copper boiler. As he poured himself a cup out he was humming a few tunes to himself awaiting his turn to be accompanied by Violet Baker on the school piano. Like a real old trouper he makes his entry past the big guns of our village, who are sitting at the top table, to be introduced properly as John Harris, bass. He is dressed in a morning suit of sorts with cloth-covered buttons, his starched shirt front partly hidden by a blue and white spotted cravat. He plomps a whole bale of music, yellow with age, on top of the piano and we look like being here all night. Just what I wanted. He waded through one piece after another, reaching depths I never thought were possible. He was a bass all right. 'Would you like a little jelly?' suggested Mrs. Collins from the shop. 'Indeed, I would, Mam,' John said, and Violet had a breather while John Harris cleared up half a bowl of raspberry jelly, the stuff just melting as the dessert spoon entered his mouth, particles clinging for a moment to his tobacco-stained walrus moustache. How long John would have sung we shall never know, for after about half an hour of these ballads of love and passion the chairman called a halt and with *Auld Lang Syne* and 'The King' sung by all, the party was over.

About twice every winter we had a magic lantern lecture in 'The Room'. There was no radio and no possibility of a visit to the pictures so these lectures were an interlude in the humdrum of school, work and bed. The magic lantern belonged to Mr. Robert Cambridge and, of course, was a carbide model. Some returned missionary would arrive with the slides and erect the screen in 'The Room'. 'Seven-thirty tonight,' read the posters, 'Mr. Blank will show pictures and describe life in an outpost of the British Empire.' At seven o'clock a few of us lads were looking through the windows of the Recreation Room while George Burford helped Mr. Howard Cambridge load the canister of the lantern with carbide and start the water dripping until a match lit the lantern and projected a yellowish light on to the screen. We filed into our seats at about seven-fifteen and sat in a group around the stove, partly because it was warm there and partly to be out of sight of the more serious-minded members who did not consider this as an entertainment but a lesson to us to appreciate the lovely surroundings we lived in under the hill. The first hymn projected on the screen, *The Church's One Foundation*, I always suspected was to make both Church and Chapel feel at home. Now came the pictures. Brown, bare bosoms of women and girls in straw skirts. The room was dark so that a titter could not be traced to any one of us, but we were not accustomed to seeing thing like this up our village street and titter we did. Men with bone skewers through their noses and sometimes the giraffe-necked women from Burma. No doubt the message was acceptable to the older members of the audience and we put our pennies in the collection, but to be honest it was the pictures we wanted and, though imperfect, they gave us something to talk about in the long dark winter. The lantern was usually reliable, but once we noticed more of a bubbling and gurgling coming from the canister holding the carbide. Then, all at once, the whole thing burst into flames right in the middle of *Greenland's Icy Mountains*, the last hymn to be projected on to the screen. George Burford turned off the gas and no harm was done.

I did mention the wireless. Well, one winter's day Sam

Green, an Evesham gramophone shopkeeper, gave a wireless concert in 'The Room'. It was a Saturday and it took all day with a forty-round ladder fixing aerials up to the end of our barn across the rickyard to the Recreation Room. Then great brown insulators were put in position. The local gravedigger volunteered to dig a sizeable hole just outside the doorway of 'The Room'. When this was done Sam Green buried an old galvanised iron bath and soldered an earth wire to this. By nightfall the three-valve wireless set with its half-hundred-weight accumulator and another dry battery was oscillating. Howard Cambridge said he knew it was going to be a wireless concert for he had been down to 'The Room' and seen the wires! When Shepherd Corbisley heard about it from John Henry and Blossom, he said 'Well, that's the master blooming job as ever I've seen or heard.' Uncle George said they 'ud upset the weather' and another old stager kept clear away, declaring it to be 'the works of the Devil'.

Other attractions or distractions at 'The Room' were Mothers' Union teas and whist drives, but there was one musical occasion which, I think, is worth mentioning. A very amateur choral society came to do or try to do *The Messiah*. They arrived, a mixed bunch from a Vale village, with two violins, the school piano, a cornet and a euphonium, together with so-called sopranos, altos, basses and tenors. Dad was in the chair. Have you ever heard hounds break cover, a pig hung in a gate, or a bumble bee in a churn? We had the lot that memorable night. There have never been such noises made in 'The Room' from that day to this. It was pathetic. It was embarrassing. To me it was funny. I wasn't old enough to feel sorry for Dad in the chair. He, a one-time bandsman in the Salvation Army, had a good ear for music. His vote of thanks was short and to the point. He thanked them for the work they had put into it. Their leader's reply was really funny. He said, 'At one time I never thought we should have been able to have done it.' They did it all right, 'Hallelujah Chorus' and all. Did we stand? I forget. Perhaps it's as well.

CHAPTER TWENTY

CHURCH AND CHAPEL

I WRITE THIS chapter with a little reluctance. Chiefly because I have a great respect for Conformist and Non-Conformist alike. The Established Church of Saint Barbara, the only one dedicated to that saint in Britain, has in my lifetime been known as Low Church and has had excellent relations with the Chapel or Free Church at the top of the village. This was not always so. Uncle Jim told me of the Reverend Joseph Harrison tolerating the Non-Conformists but describing their open air meetings as entertainments. The Reverend Harrison was a friend of the poor but he had to toe the line to the Squire. He was a thirsty man and when he ran short of money at Christmas would accept two pounds ten from my grandfather for the rent of some glebe land due at Ladyday, when the sum owing would have been three pounds. The pew ends were a great help to him when he became a bit unsteady but his doctrine was 'Don't do as I do. Do as I tell you.' At one wedding he was halfway through with the funeral service before he realised his mistake. He apologised to the couple, explaining that he was 'so filled with the spirit'.

Non-conformity in Ashton can be traced back to 1645, to the time of Richard Edes, a friend of Richard Baxter of Kidderminster. But we will start with overflowing meetings in Mr. Steel's cottage; it was necessary to find more room in Sam Merril's barn at New Farm. In June 1881 a Mr. Ball held a mission there and gained a number of converts, and in November of that year a mission room was opened sponsored by the Evesham Evangelistic Band, the Bomfords and others of the same persuasion.

It's often been said of the old-time local preacher that he 'preached hell fire until you could almost smell the brimstone'. My father told me of Jim Haines from Evesham who took off his coat and rolled up his sleeves to preach his sermon. They were termed 'Bible thumpers' or 'ranters' but were in the main dedicated men who spoke from the heart. But in religion there is always a fanatic fringe. The keeping of the Sabbath was similar to the way it is in the Western Isles of Scotland today. Ben Madement from Grafton had his Sunday boots cleaned by his boys on Saturday nights. One Saturday they forgot to clean them and he caught them cleaning them on Sunday morning. 'Stop!' he said, after one boot had been cleaned; and he went to Chapel with one boot blacked and one dirty.

Early in this century two Ashton farmers who were neighbours fell out or, to use the local expression, 'dropped out'. Both were Anglicans and one especially hated the 'ranters'. A travelling Evangelist could not find anywhere to pitch his tent. Then one farmer welcomed him into his orchard. The villagers said, 'What's gone wrong with old Freddy?' But the orchard was just opposite the front door of his neighbour and he thought the singing and the noise would annoy his neighbour. The result— about twenty converts to Non-Conformity. By this time open-air meetings, often wrongly timed and badly sited, were reinforced by the Salvation Army band.

Freddy's neighbour was an autocrat of the old school, the so-called guardian of the poor who offered two and sixpence for Parish Relief or the House (the workhouse or grubber). He took delight in trying to break up open-air meetings. On one occasion at the top of Pig Lane a Salvation Army officer from Winchcombe, a former prize fighter known locally as Toad Pelt, was praying with a little ring of followers. The guardian of the poor walked through the ring and jostled Toad Pelt with his shoulder. Like a flash Toad Pelt hit him on the nose and invited anyone else who felt like it into the ring, adding these words from the Bible, 'As the churning of milk bringeth forth butter so does the ringing of the nose bring forth blood'.

Toleration was completely lacking. There were faults on both sides. Statements were made at some open-air meetings, intentionally or not, which added fuel to the flames and upset the Anglicans. On the other side, one of the Squire's keepers threw half a brick through the Mission Hall window, striking an old lady on the head. Since 1912 the relations between Church and Chapel in our village have been cordial. Miss Millie Bostock, a very strong Anglican, gave recitals on the Free Church organ to raise money. The Chapel people attended the special efforts for the Anglican Church and so forth.

I did not realise until quite recently that some of the old local preachers at the Chapel practised the Welsh Hywel. Edward Roberts (blacksmith) from Evesham was a Welshman, a dwarf for a blacksmith. He was so short that the top part of the pulpit had to be dismantled when he preached or else we could only see the top of Edward's head. Sitting in the second seat from the front I didn't miss much. The flowers had to be moved also, to a side table by a tablet in memory of Thomas Jones.

Don't call me over-critical. These men did their best. I do remember the unorthodox, the mistakes men made, but as a boy with an enquiring mind that was just me. Edward, after mopping his brow of perspiration (he'd had a hard ride from Evesham), began with these words, 'Let us commence our service with prayer'. One example of Edward's Hywel was when he half sang and half said, 'Jeremiah—was called—the Doleful Prophet—because he wrote the book of Lamentations.' I remember him speaking of the folly of a hurried meal. 'Some people say that every time we speak we miss a mouthful but I think mealtimes should be times of conversation.' Edward was one who prayed for 'our friends at St. Barbara's and all worshipping in like manner in spirit and in truth'. Before my time Enoch Bygraves spoke for an hour on, 'Jonah was in the whale's belly three days and three nights'. A farmer from Beckford took for his subject, 'We are the brothers'. Tom Adams on the Monday went to see him and said, 'You remember what you said about all us being brothers last night?' The farmer said, 'Yes, Tom, I do.' 'Could you lend me forty pounds then?' said Tom. Charlie Bradfield said, 'Oi, but he wasn't brother enough for that.' George Barnet from Broadway is reputed to have announced, 'Hymn number ticty-tix in Tankey's Tongs and Tolos, "Id dat tumbody du?"'

In between the dour, the amusing, we had a few excellent speakers. There was a devout man from Pershore, Reuben Broad. We knew what his subject would be—Shadrach, Meshach and Abednego in the burning fiery furnace. He was a tall dark-skinned man with closely cropped hair and a heart as good as gold. I could tell you of lots of people he helped through difficult times. He referred to us as 'Ma friends'. Once he forgot to take his cycle clips off his trousers and as he paced the platform did this without interrupting his address. Another hot summer Sunday he came without waistcoat and, with his thumbs linked under his elastic braces, drew the braces forward one at a time to be released like a catapult against his chest. His prayer was a gem, always the same. (Who said we have no ritual?) He started off, 'Lord, remember all who worship Thee, tonight, not only in the cathedrals, the temples, the tabernacles and fine churches throughout the length and breadth of our land, but in the chapels, little Bethels and under the canopy of the glorious Heavens; in fact, in every small corner of Thy great vineyard.'

One visiting preacher who shouted, laughed and cried, and rampaged up and down the platform, kicked the collection basket for six up the aisle, just missing me. He shouted, 'Filthy lucre!' and George Foster replied. 'Hallelujah!' He was one of the few old-timers who practised 'button-holing'. This was done by the preacher quietly leaving the stage during the singing of the benediction hymn and being in position in the porch to tackle any likely-looking sinner. His boots squeaked as he passed me. Then he popped the question in the porch. 'Are you on the Lord's side?' I think it did more harm than good as it kept people away.

When the Reverend Harry Soan was Baptist minister at Atch Lench and Dunnington, he came over to our village chapel and took the service. He brought with him a note of optimism which had a special appeal for us boys. He organised one of the first boys' clubs at his village. Among the wit that was skilfully mingled with his message, I remember a tale he told. A nobleman was coming to stay at a large house where a small boy had just been engaged as pantry boy. The butler gave the boy instructions to take shaving water up to the nobleman's bedroom in the morning. He was to knock at the door and when asked who was there to reply, 'It's the boy, my Lord, with the shaving water.' The boy rehearsed this, but when the moment came made the awful mistake of replying, 'It's the Lord, my boy, with the shaving water.' The Reverend Harry Soan was then, and still is, a great character.

Tom Wheatcroft told me of one man who came from Tewkesbury to preach and declared he had 'a peace as calm as the troubled ocean'. He also warned the congregation, 'If you don't repent you'll be working for the devil with a wooden pick and shovel digging taters by the bushel on the turnpike road.'

Fred Bushell came from Cleeve Prior way on his bike. His face shone with human kindness. His address was a series of tales and experiences. His constant theme was how we could help one another and how ordinary people had helped him. He'd start off, 'I remember one time when I was in Birmingham.' After the meeting, a Quaker meeting, I gather, someone said to him, 'What did you think of the doctor this morning?' He said, 'Very good, but it was that old labourer who opened his heart that gave me the blessing.' 'Did I ever tell you about the time I went to Canada?' he went on. 'We were in mid-Atlantic at ten o'clock on the Sunday morning when the pianist was playing music-hall stuff. I said to the Captain, "Couldn't we have something more appropriate for Sunday morning?" The Captain said, "You carry on," so I distributed some hymn books and I had got my cornet with me and I asked the company to pick a favourite hymn. One man said, "Can we have 'Now the day is over'?" We sang it at ten o'clock in the morning and I don't know as ever I heard it sung any better.' He was a great character, always emphasising that we had a lot to be thankful for.

Services of song could be amusing. At one such service the ladies sang, 'Oh for a man, oh for a man, or for a mansion in the skies.' The men replied, 'Lord send sal, Lord send sal, Lord send salvation to our hearts.'

Tom Wheatcroft told me of the preachers of years ago, unlearned, uneducated, but full of enthusiasm. One such man asked the question, 'Why did God make Eve out of Adam's rib? If you don't know I'll tell ya. If he had a-made her out of Adam's arm or Adam's leg, Adam would have been dependent on the Parish for relief for the rest of his life.'

Tom and Bill Windsor, father and son, were both good honest men. Tom rode an ancient tricycle and Bill had a motorcycle. 'Capital, capital!' was Tom's favourite expression. Bill used words I didn't understand, like 'Dynamic debauchery', but I do remember his usual text, 'Our light affliction, which is just for a moment, is nothing compared with the glory which is to come.' He brought with him the Bidford Nightingale, a counter tenor, to sing falsetto solos which I tried to copy after my voice broke.

These were our preachers. They were ably supported by an orchestra of bass viol, cello, two violins, and sometimes a piano accordeon. The honorary secretary when he gave the notices out gave a little sermon as well. He didn't know quite when to stop. The Christmas treat was announced as follows, 'Well, friends, you are all invited to our annual tea in the Recreation Room on Wednesday. That includes the koyr, the Sunday school, anyone who has ever taken an interest in this place. The tea will commence at approximately about half past five, I should think. (It never started until six p.m.) But I'd like the ladies (broad smile) to be there in good time to get the tea because you all knows what it says in the Word. "The night commeth when no mon can work".'

The tea drinkers packed the room, and after Christmas puddings with threepenny bits in and the usual brew out of the urns, games began, all the usual—'Sir Roger', 'A-hunting we will go', 'Clap and run' and 'Spinning the trencher'. As the party warmed up Mr. Carter came through the door with the strongest waggon rope he could find and a tug-of-war took place in the room until more often than not the winners landed on the stage or down the steps, or the rope broke. We stayed until about ten o'clock when some of the broader-minded chapel members suggested, 'Let's have a jig round' and, would you believe it, dancing commenced. Mr. Carter didn't object and he paid for the tea so, like David of old, they danced.

The two churches are still fairly strong and as old Tom Wheatcroft told me, 'The Chapel a-gin you a good staddle (foundation) and you a-got to pick the meat off the bones.'

CHAPTER TWENTY-ONE

CHRISTMAS, THE BELL RINGERS AND MILLIE BOSTOCK

SQUIRE BOSWORTH, his bailiffs and his men took very little notice of 25th December as Christmas Day. They celebrated Old Christmas Day, 6th January. The men had a holiday on this day and the farmers and gentry held a sparrow shoot in the field opposite the White Hart. The sparrows were released from traps and the sport was similar to the clay pigeon shoots of today. The place was alive with bookies and tic tac men, who shouted the odds two to one on the bird or three to one on the gun. The only way the labouring classes were involved in this was that the Squire's steam-engine driver, Davis, and old Oliver had several nights out bird batting previous to Christmas, catching the sparrows with a net and attracting them with a lantern while little boys beat the hedges and ricks with sticks. The sparrows were kept in a wire cage at Shaw Green until the shoot. I suspect that any other birds which they caught and which were edible made puddings and pies for the bird batters. The workpeople also had their plum puddings, cooked in a cloth in their copper boilers, on Christmas Day.

Skipping many years, my first recollections of Christmas were the bells ringing before daybreak on 21st December, St. Thomas's morning, and the little boys singing in the half-light, 'Here we come a-Thomasin', a-Thomasin', a-Thomasin', Here we come a-Thomasin', so early in the morning'. They were singing for pennies.

What of Christmas Day for us? Sugar mice in our stockings. Sucking pig for dinner. The flocks of carol singers. A sack bag of oranges in the hall to give them. Christmas puddings hooked out by the string from our copper boiler, using a toasting fork. The smell of steam. The size of the raisins. On Christmas after-

noon we had a visit from the Tewkesbury Drum and Fife Band.
I was fascinated with this and Tom Wheatcroft, who was with
the cows in the yard, about to milk or 'draw the blessing', as he
called it, said, 'Oi, we a got the tabber and tut come agun.' The
wind howled up our chimney as the kettle swung on the pot
hook over our oven grate in the kitchen one Christmas and Dad
remarked how bad it was for those at sea. Then he told us of big
freeze ups when a pig was roasted on the frozen Avon at
Evesham and Grandfather Westwood skated to Tewkesbury.
Men could tag on behind the threshing drum from farm to
farm if they were lucky and provided their own shuppick (fork).
Some took to poaching; some sold herrings, walking around
the villages. We felt thankful for a good roof and plenty of little
luxuries.

Boxing Day was a grand shooting day for us. The rabbits
caught were sent to Evesham workhouse to give the inmates
rabbit pie suppers. I recall one such day on the hill, when some
of Mr. Carter's and Dad's friends from Evesham kept up a
continual barrage. The cartridges, Crimson Flash, came in
hundreds from Barrats, near Evesham river bridge. I was lucky
when one stray pellet ricocheted off a stone wall and drilled a
hole through the top of my ear. After we had changed we all
went to Mr. Carter's to a lovely tea, chocolate blancmange with
a lion on the top of the mould, lots of trifle, jellies of all flavours
and pink celery. Mr. Carter grew some crisp pink celery which
was rather noisy as we sat around his big dining table eating it.
The tea was strong and I liked it that way. I believe Mr. Carter
bought it in bulk in chests. He was the sort of man who bought
in bulk : trucks of coal at the station, soap in large quantities
and huge blocks of salt. He thought big and he bought big.
After the usual crackers we played 'Pit', a game which can get
very noisy. Miss Carter's young man got very boisterous as he
shouted 'Come on Barley'.

Mr. Carter had laid by a good stock of walnuts off the five
trees in his rickyard and with a brass top we played 'Put and
take' for them. It doesn't sound awfully Chapel but I won a lot
of walnuts one Christmas. No, it didn't start me backing

horses. Uncle Jim said the only time he backed a horse was through a shop window, and when he could see the bookmakers walking the roads with the seat out of their trousers and the backers driving their posh cars, he'd think there was something in it.

At about seven o'clock on Boxing Night the Evesham Salvation Army Band formed up on Mr. Carter's lawn. Both he and Dad had been in the band and made them welcome. I don't honestly think there are many things more stirring than to hear the Army play carols on a clear, crisp, frosty night. We stood on the front steps, the acetylene lamp hanging from a pole in the midst of the group, and heard the familiar old tunes, 'Who is he in yonder stall?' What would Christmas have been without it?

Back in the drawing room Mr. Carter had put the butt of a hawthorn tree on the open fire. As we sat snugly round and carried on eating the mince pies, the band left. Dad said to Mr. Carter, 'Do you remember that winter, Harry, when we were out playing carols with the band?' 'Yes, Tom, I do, and it almost froze our breath that night. Instruments, Tom! I had to keep a bar of soap in my tunic pocket to fill the holes up in my euphonium, but we were about forty strong then.'

We left Mr. Carter's at about eight-thirty p.m. and were in our kitchen at home getting ready for bed when a knock came at the door and Walt in a stage whisper enquired, 'Be the little uns gone to bed?' The bell ringers had arrived and we were not in bed. 'Shall we sing you a couple of carols, Mam?' Mother said, 'Certainly, Walt. Having a good Christmas?' Walt said, 'Oi, but I ca'unt sing like I used to years agu.' By the light of Walt's stable lantern hung on a forked stick, the five ringers started. Job Wheatcroft on crutches (he'd lost a leg at Mons) gave the note. He had a deep bass voice. They sang, *All Hail and Praise, the Sacred Morn*, then *Arise, Ye Sleepy Souls, Arise*. These two pieces were local carols, and until a few years before, they had sung another local one, the Withy carol. Lastly, the *pièce de résistance* came—*While Shepherds Watched*, to the tune Lyneham. I have never heard carol singing like it; it was so sincere. It could have been the first Christmas.

On New Year's Eve the ringers rang the old year out with a buff or muffled peal, Old Lofty having had to climb among the bells to fix the leather mufflers. When the New Year came in, a merry peal was rung and the ringers fired the bells, ringing them all at once like the guns in the 1812 Overture.

Millie Bostock, after carols had been sung at turned midnight, invited the ringers through her house, the darkest, Job Wheatcroft, first, and with wine and mince pies warmed them and wished them a Happy New Year.

Millie Bostock was a kindly woman; she did a tremendous lot of good. I can see her now taking bowls of soup, jelly and blancmanges to sick poor people. She played the church organ, but did seem to make it resound with *The Dead March in Saul*. Once Oliver was down with lumbago. He wouldn't have the doctor so Millie, who was a very amateur nurse, having once worked in a doctor's house, put some sort of plaster on his back which fetched quite a bit of skin off and Oliver was not at all pleased. Millie boasted she had more bones in the churchyard than anyone in the village. She lived in one of our cottages and we looked forward to her coming over to pay her rent, which took the whole evening. She was a spinster of sixty plus. We heard about her love affairs; how she nearly married the captain of Evesham Fire Brigade, then a music master from Stratford-upon-Avon. She said, 'All young men should have a spell in the army to straighten their backs.' She was a keen gardener; she also ran the Mothers' Union. Millie was a practical Christian in every way.

CHAPTER TWENTY-TWO

NOTEWORTHY MEN OF ASHTON

I SUPPOSE SOMEONE somewhere ploughs or digs up something interesting from the past every day. In Ashton I have found bits of Roman pottery smashed by that monster, the gyro-tiller. Coins are unearthed in gardens and this is commonplace. In 1900 the late Mr. James Cotton was gardening at Higford House and he found a Porto Bello medal. Here is an extract from *The Evesham Journal* of the time: 'The medal is in good condition; it was struck in 1739, is in bronze and commemorates Admiral Vernon's victory over the Spaniards with six ships at Porto Bello.' It is said that Admiral Vernon lived for a time at Higford House, a massive manor type of house with a stone ball on each gatepost. The seaman's chest, which was in St. Barbara's Church until lately, inscribed R.N., is supposed to have belonged to him. He was nicknamed "Old Grog" by the sailors of his day for his coat of grogram, silk and mohair. He introduced rum into the Navy as an antidote to scurvy. Rum is still known as grog today in the Royal Navy after Admiral Vernon.

Just over the parish boundary, a rippling stream flows off the hill which is crossed by a little footbridge; the footpath leads to Grafton. John Drinkwater, the Midland poet, described Grafton as it was before the 1914 war in one of his poems. I would not add to that except that no house or cottage has been built there this century and it remains today very much as he saw it.

Just as the twentieth century dawned, Professor Alfred Hayes, scholar, writer and dramatist, lived at Grafton in a house directly opposite the thatched cottage which was once a small church. The Norman arch of its former chancel can still be seen. It was built by the monks of Beckford Priory. Professor

Hayes translated drama in verse from the Russian of Pushkin. His other works included *A Fellowship of Song* and a historical drama about Simon de Montfort. This was in verse.

But more about the great man himself. He loved his garden and tutored his students in Russian on the lawn. If the weather was chilly, he would wrap a plaid blanket around his shoulders. His costume plays were often rehearsed in his garden to the delight of the native people, 'the sons of the soil' of this hamlet. Mrs. Hayes had a lovely singing voice and would sing for hours to the accompaniment of Sir Granville Bantock on the grand piano. Sir Granville, a frequent visitor to the Hayes household, had particular distinction as a composer but most of all for his instrumentation. He regarded himself as an individualist and didn't worry in the least about what was the popular music of the day. His *Helena Variations for Orchestra* were written in honour of his wife and he set some of her poems to music. Sibelius dedicated his third symphony to him.

Sir Granville's hobbies were simple. A burly, bearded man, he enjoyed nothing better than a day's trout fishing with Alfred Hayes in the Elan Valley and bringing home the catch to their Birmingham house for Annie Spiers to cook for their supper.

What colourful personalities these two were! Alfred Hayes's garden was a delightful spot under the hill, where he grew rare plants and flowers and planted a walnut tree, not half grown. The hill above Grafton was as a classroom before him where he studied another interest, geology. He enjoyed the simple life, mixing with the farmers and labourers, who felt equally at home in his company. Sir Granville, constantly improvising on the grand piano, amused Annie Spiers as she worked in the kitchen and heard softly whispered from the drawing room, '1–2–3–4, 1–2–3–4' as he played a new setting. His son practised on the bagpipes in the lane outside. Can you imagine the comments? Had ever such an instrument been heard in Grafton before?

It's good to cast the mind back to those peaceful days. Visitors arriving at Ashton station from Birmingham, little Martin Hawker meeting the train with a hand cart, loading it up with their trunks and boxes and pushing his cargo a mile

and a half from the station to Grafton, the last half mile being
uphill. Martin earned his mug of cider at the end of his journey.

About this time my father grew strawberries in a field we
called 'Up Lenchwick', and while working there he met another
great man who came to live at Grafton, Dr. L. P. Jacks. Dr.
Jacks took a liking to Dad and bought strawberries from him.
He also tried to persuade Dad to go to Canada to manage a
farm for him. As a philosopher, essayist and editor, Dr. Jacks
was world famous. He was minister of the Church of the Messiah at Birmingham and Principal of Manchester College at
Oxford, a centre of Unitarianism. He came to Grafton to live at
the Middle Farm, a little lower down the hill from Professor
Hayes. As keepers of bees and fruit growers they had much in
common. Harold Begbee described him as 'a man with a nobly-
coloured ivory face ploughed up and furrowed by mental strife'.
His head was crowned with white hair. An outdoor man, he was
short, thick-set with heavy shoulders, deep chest, and the slow
movements of a peasant. Dr. Jacks married Olive Cecilia,
daughter of the Reverend Stopford Brook, in 1889. She was a
most beautiful woman and was a model for quite a well known
painting, *The Gardener's Daughter*.

Dr. Jacks kept an Italian variety of bees. The beehives were in
Dr. Jacks' garden among the apple trees opposite his house.
Adjoining his garden was a meadow belonging to the Middle
Farm. Tom Wheatcroft at that time was a carter there. The
meadow was for mowing and haymaking this one year and
Tom, a young carter with lively young horses, was worried
about these bees being so close to the mowing grass. 'Warm
assed uns,' he called the bees. When mowing-time arrived Tom
was up before daybreak and had mowed half the field before the
farmer arrived in the morning. The farmer said, 'What's up a
thee this morning, Thomas? Couldn't sleep?' Tom knew what
he was about. He wanted the job done before the bees got up.
Neither he nor his horses got stung.

Two more Ashton men were not so lucky. Old Allen and
Spider had been on the cider and Dr. Jacks had asked them to

move some of his empty beehives in the garden and put them under the hedge. They caught hold of one full of bees, fell over with it and pulled the hive on top of them. They got badly stung but soon became sober. When Dr. Jacks moved from Grafton he had a hundred fruit trees which he had planted in his garden. These were now nearly half grown. He was determined to take them with him to Headington, near Oxford, where he was going to live. Little Martin Hawker carefully dug up all these trees, wrapped the roots in sacking, took them to Beckford station a few at a time in John Crump's waggon, and loaded them in trucks for Headington. This meant many journeys for the trees took up a lot of room. Martin planted them at Headington and I believe they all grew. Martin was a man we shall never see the like of again. The bees . . . they went too. Dr. Jacks could do anything with them.

He remained a strong character until his death at the good old age of ninety-five. Grafton, without doubt, inspired some of his books. If you read *Mad Shepherds*, that part of Bredon Hill seems to come to life.

While Dr. Jacks was at Grafton he and Professor Hayes added distinction to the Harvest Homes they attended in John Crump's big barn. Everyone was expected to take part on these social occasions. Mr. John Crump held one memorable Harvest Home after a good harvest during the Boer War. One of the dances, called 'The Rose Basket', was danced accompanied by the waving of handkerchiefs. Mr. Hayes and John Drinkwater took great interest in the rustic tunes and while together at Grafton visited Beckford Inn and listened to the quaint songs of the pea-pickers and gypsies and 'dotted' the tune and words down in the bar as the songs were sung. Back to the Harvest Home in John Crump's barn. Charles Spiers, grandfather of Annie Spiers, was born in 1812; today remembered more by Tschaikovsky's overture than by Napoleon's retreat from Moscow, he had a special part in the harvest entertainment. After *Sweet Annie Benbow* had been sung by one and all, Charles recited:

'All ye rakish farmers that stay up late at night.
Mind when you go to bed to choose some candlelight.
Now, Betty, you go up to bed,
And I'll stay up tonight instead.'

Songs by Mrs. Hayes and her son, Mr. Robin Hayes, who also
had a good voice, mingled with *The Spotted Cow* and *The
Sweet Nightingale*, the latter a part song joined in by the
carters, shepherds, cowmen and daymen. Annie Spiers's father
played the melodeon; others mouth organs. Home-made cider
from John Crump's Black Tauntons quenched the thirst, and as
Little Martin said, 'there was allus plenty of fittle including
Michaelmas goose.' Various toasts were proposed. One used
was:

'The Plough and the Frail,
The Fleece and the Flail,
Not forgetting the Milking Pail.'

Our first Grafton character was John Drinkwater, one of the
great rural poets of the century. We will finish with a few of his
lines:

'The days are good at Grafton,
The golden days and grey,
The busy clouds, the mellow barns,
And every winding way;
And oh, the peace of Grafton
Beneath the starlit skies.
God dreamt of when he fashioned
A woman's love-lit eyes.'

CHAPTER TWENTY-THREE

BREAST PLOUGHS, SQUITCH AND SUPERSTITION

A LOT HAS been written and said about the market gardener in the 1890s and early years of the twentieth century in our Vale of Evesham. What sort of picture does he conjure up in our minds? Some would have us believe he grew his crops entirely on stable and pig manure, that he had hardly any pests and diseases in his crops, and that, apart from the late spring frosts which killed all his fruit some years, the produce of his ground had more flavour and goodness than it has today.

Pests and diseases were not unknown to the old gardener; he had his own ways of dealing with them. How was the clean top accomplished? Firstly, in the 1890s, by breast ploughing after crops of peas, beans, etc., were over; then by burning all the breast-ploughed stubbles. All patches of squitch (couch grass) were dug and burnt in March. These fires burned for days. The middle was raked out each morning with a 'scatter' which blacksmiths made from a four-tine fork with the tines turned at right angles.

This scorched-earth policy was sound. The gardener had a theory that pests and diseases lurked in the hollow stalks of beans and corn crops. The burning of sprout and cabbage stumps or stems destroyed aphids, the fly- or flea-beetles. Many pictures have been painted of the horse team at plough—a pleasant sight—but to see the old gardener with his two-tine digger or two-pronged fork cranked by the local blacksmith to suit his physique, every spit which he dug falling in the exact spot he intended, was a picture indeed.

I know one of these corn gardeners who came to live in our village—Sam from Evesham. He wore cord trousers, yorks, with the inevitable peg tucked under one of them to clean his tools,

and an Oxford shirt without collar summer and winter. In very
hard weather he wore a muffler around his neck. (Incidentally,
a young man in our village was unable to obtain work on the
land because he wore a collar and tie.) Sam had hard, horny
hands, the result of contact with crude tools. He bought a two-
tine fork for two and ninepence in 1897 and planted a part of
his six acres with strawberries and some with asparagus. He said
that with these crops 'you got no seedsmen to pay every year'.
So small was the margin of profit that at first he carried his
asparagus in a hamper to within two miles of Evesham market
or just over halfway and then went the rest of the journey by
train. Others pushed their hand-carts to distant stations, bringing back their empty hampers.

The asparagus price was so low one year that some gardeners
threw the bundles of asparagus into the Avon at Evesham Workman Bridge, while others fished them out again at Hampton
Ferry. Sam's strawberries saved him, and when asked by the
vicar of our parish how he lived, he replied, 'I've got my well
and the ravens feed me like they did Elijah.'

When my old friend first took over his holding he noticed a
patch of clover which kept green all the summer. That was
where he sank his never-failing well. He was an individualist; he
sowed his harvesting onion seed broadcast; he used a saucer to
put Peruvian guano to his lettuce; he planted his potatoes a
yard square, and with heavy manuring and soot produced
enormous crops. Picking up a potato on Redditch railway platform he took it home, cut it into several pieces, planted them
and kept the strain for years, naming it 'Redditch Platform'.

The squitch fires of March with the burnt stems and earth
produced quantities of red ashes, and when this was mixed with
pig manure and the contents of the earth closet and dug into
the ground, it held the crops in a dry summer. But the gardener
was quick to realise the benefits of mineral fertilisers which he
always called 'artificial'. Kainite for asparagus was fifty shillings
per ton in 1891. Blue acid sulphate of ammonia from the local
gas works and nitrate of soda were both cheap. One grower put
it this way: 'Nitrogen is nitrogen whether it comes from Chile

or out of a Hereford bull.'

The old gardeners' tools were chosen for various jobs with as much care as a golfer would choose his club for a difficult shot out of the rough. Peas were set with home-made setting pins but some were planted with a tool called a channelor and scuffed in with hobnailed boots, which amounted to almost another tool. Gardeners were continually improvising. In 1894 my grandfather hitched his donkey to his breast plough. But mainly the work was mauling from seed-time to harvest. Larkworthy's of Worcester and Burlinghams of Evesham produced a two-wheeled skim suitable for one horse. This to a large extent replaced the breast plough and took some of the back-ache out of producing the clean top.

In 1907 watches were set by Beech's hooter, used for the jam factory. All gardeners were weather prophets of sorts. By 1908 weather forecasts were printed in the local paper, but 'That train sound holla'. We're in for a change', and 'It'll rain when the sun gets down along with the wind', were common expressions. Then, of course, there was the annual ritual of Clark's Hill to see where the wind was at twelve o'clock on the 21st March and there it was supposed to stay for three months. The market gardeners made this annual trek without question, probably finishing up with a day for the Queen.

Superstitions remained with some old gardeners, who would plant seeds only when the moon was waxing. Broad beans were planted near gooseberry bushes to keep away the mildew, and gilly flowers between seville beans to keep away the fly- or flea-beetle.

Sprays were used in 1900. Bordeaux mixture containing copper sulphate paris green was sown to kill leather grubs. But in Sam's words, 'It's better to spray the roots and keep the crop growing with good manure.' It's a sobering thought that had Bordeaux mixture been available in the 1840s, thousands would not have died in the Irish Potato Famine.

It took my father all day to take his produce to Evesham market with his donkey and cart and collect his empty hampers. Giberts of Evesham made spring carts for the men who had ponies, but Dad told me that sometimes the braying of the donkeys stopped the auction sale in Evesham market. Dad's donkey refused to trot after dark, and it was a long ride home, six miles on a winter's evening. If a leaf rustled in the hedge or a bird moved, Neddy laid his long ears forward just to find out what it was and would not budge.

Our friend Sam had his cider made at the cider mill at Hampton which, apart from producing cider, produced pomace which the gardeners dug in. The apple pips germinated and the young suckers were budded with the popular varieties of the day. Some of these trees have only recently been uprooted.

CHAPTER TWENTY-FOUR

HARVESTING THEN AND NOW

VILLAGE LIFE, work, sport and characters over the last hundred years, particularly in our little group of houses nestled under the hill at Ashton, has been our subject so far. I want now to consider some of the changes that have taken place.

When it comes to counting heads, there has been very little change in the population of our village over the past hundred years. The census of 1861 showed a population of four hundred and eleven in Ashton-under-Hill for an acreage of eighteen hundred. The 1961 figure is four hundred and thirty inhabitants. So little change? Well, we shall see. Harvest time is perhaps the most appropriate season for looking at changes in village life.

I said we had four hundred and thirty inhabitants. How do they earn their bread? Well, thirty-one men and boys work full time on the land today and a number of women do seasonal work. Twelve school teachers live here. Where there was once the sound at morning and evening of the tread of hob-nailed boots passing up and down the village, today there is the noise of cars, buses and motor bikes taking the majority of the people to work in factories, offices and so forth. In fact we are witnessing the biggest revolution in village life since the time of the enclosures and its gathering momentum.

Look at Ashton again. Morris's 'Directory of Gloucestershire' for 1867 listed seven farmers in the village, one blacksmith, one wheelwright, a parish clerk, one tailor and shopkeeper, three bear retailers and one carrier. The latter plied to Evesham on Mondays and Cheltenham on Saturdays. These were the trades and professions. There were also four people listed as gentry. We must assume that the remainder of the workers were employed by these people. What did they do?

Let us imagine the harvest scene of a hundred years ago in the light of what we know about conditions and customs then.

A good man could cut with two hooks (bagging hook and pick thank) an acre of corn a day, with his wife and children tying it up for him with straw bands. These were the days when the harvest called for all the available man-power of the village. The condition of the grain was so important to the villagers that a wet harvest meant poor quality bread, the dough running about the oven.

Harvesting in those days before the machine took charge was a quiet ingathering which depended upon the partnership of man, horse and steam. A good day's work for three horses, one man, and a boy to ride the foremost horse, would be to cut and tie into sheaves ten acres of corn with the binder. If three horses were abreast on the binders, the boy was not needed and less time was wasted turning the machine at the corners. Sometimes the farmer was anxious to finish cutting a large field in one day in order to kill the rabbits, so as the binder ate its way into the crop the horses were periodically changed and the machine was kept going all day. In a long day sixteen acres could be cut. Tractors with two men have cut twenty acres plus in a day. With the binder, though, we must not forget that one man was needed to cut the road round the headlands and two men to stack the sheaves up in the aisles, thus making it safe to withstand a storm or two. Then we have the pitchers and loaders, two of each loading the waggon in what was known as boat fashion. One was loading the front up high and the other was at the back, leaving the middle of the boat at a lower level to suit the pitchers. The middle of the waggon was loaded last after being used as a platform to receive the sheaves. Then there was a boy to lead the horses in the ground and a carter to haul to and from the rick. That made ten men and one boy.

At the rick we have one man to unload the waggon, another standing on the edge of the rick (or on the roof) and two men on the rick, one binding and the other dropping the sheaves conveniently butt end first. Here there is a team of fourteen men and one boy and we have enough to complete the building of the rick, apart from thatching it. Threshing by steam, if the job was to go smoothly, needed three men tossing the sheaves off the rick, butt ends first, to the bond cutter who stood on the threshing machine cutting the strings and dropping the cut sheaves in front of the man feeding the drum. The latter's job was to maintain a constant flow of unthreshed corn going into the threshing drum, and he did this with a short shuppick. Another man pitched the boltings of threshed straw to two men building the straw rick. Another man was busy wheeling the sacks of corn into the granary on a sack cart as they came off the machine. Yet another man was carrying rowens (or broken straw) into the barn in a sheet made of sacking. Then there was a youth carrying chaff in the same way, while another with yokes and buckets kept the steam engine supplied with water. Here there is a team of twelve men and youths. It could be done by fewer men, but a daily output of one hundred sacks of wheat or eleven tons five hundred weight was aimed at.

Now consider the contrast after a hundred years. The present method of harvesting we all know. Shall we call it 'gorging'? A skilled mechanic in a boiler suit rides his combine harvester like a great ocean liner. It consumes the standing corn at the rate of about three acres an hour. A fourteen foot model threshes seven tons an hour and is operated by one man. In perfect conditions nine tons an hour have been dealt with by a British machine. The grain tank it carries holds seventy-seven bushels. It discharges its cargo into a tipping trailer down a spout at the rate of one bushel per second.

If the haul is not too long one man hauls the grain and tips his trailer load into a pit, from where it is elevated to storage bins or put through a drier first, according to the moisture content.

There are two men doing the whole operation—

'Where once the broad-wheeled waggon rumbled in,
Now this great contraption made of tin.'

Another man with a pick-up baler deals with the straw. This, when baled, is picked up by one man with hydraulic equipment.

The drift from the land has been news for so long that it is accepted. Industry offers more money and shorter hours. That is one reason why men leave the land. There is another, which many fail to realise. Farm work is a lonelier life than it was when men worked in teams. There was more fellowship in the old days as men ate their bait together under a shady tree. As William Barnes put it,

> 'There do I vind it stir my heart,
>   To hear the frothèn hosses snort.'

The combine harvester of 1965 is again the Solitary Reaper of 1803:

> 'Behold her, single in the field.'

Could Wordsworth have imagined how lonely reaping could become?

CHAPTER TWENTY-FIVE

THE CHANGING PATTERN

SINCE THE death of our last squire in 1895 the farmland has been divided up into individual farms occupied by working farmers. There was an exception. A John Bosworth, a distant relative to the late squire, continued for a time as a hunting and shooting man and was what would be termed today an autocrat. At the squire's death the land had reached a low ebb. Tom Wheatcroft told me that Squire Bosworth sacked his best 'bailey' (bailiff), who lived in my present house; the bailey was told bluntly by the Lord of the Manor. 'I don't like the colour of thee hair.' (It was red, so was the squire's.) Oliver, the shepherd, Uncle Jim and Tom Wheatcroft all told me that the time to live in the country was before the 1914 war and it's never been the same since. They are all gone, and as every year passes fewer of the people remember these times. Good work is being done literally digging up the past and learning about ancient civilisation. But characters die, ways of life are forgotten, and sayings and dialects go with them.

> Our life is a dream,
> Our time as a stream
> Glides swiftly away,
> And the fugitive moment refuses to stay.

Sam from Asum (Evesham), our first market gardener, came to our village soon after the squire's death and rented glebe land from the Church. He kept his pony in the Rope Ground, a small field set aside. The rent went to provide St. Barbara's with bell ropes. Sam and Mr. Carter, another Evesham man, brought knowledge of market gardening to our village. Mr. Carter, who joined forces with Dad, was in his element gardening. There was always a chance of a piece of peas or runner beans selling in a scarce year. As sprouts became more of a main crop and wheat growing became 'not woth the candle', as Shepherd Corbisley said, the pattern of life changed. Blenheim, bent back, his cord trousers yorked up, was hoeing sprouts down the Groaten when he remarked to me, 'This parish stinks a sprouts.' 'What's going in that field next year, Blenheim?' I said. 'Oi, sprouts agin like enough. What else can our gaffer plant? It's no good planting wait (wheat). You can buy it at seven bob a hundred at Brown's at Asum. And dost thee know what Careful Billy brought me? Half a hundred a sharps (middlings) for my pig and made a special journey from Beckford. I'll be dalled if we shaunt all look like sprouts.'

'How much wait a thee fayther planted this year, Frederick?' he added. I had to admit only one acre in the Thurness and this was cone wheat, a bearded variety. If we had planted any other sort the sparrows would have eaten the lot. This was in the late twenties and was the only wheat that year in the parish. We grew it for the straw to thatch the hay ricks. Tom Wheatcroft treated the straw like gold and littered the cattle yard in winter with rough hay.

Stocky Hill had to turn from the yearly routine of corn growing to pea-hoeing and keeping the pigeons off the sprouts with his twelve-bore gun in winter. I told him one day that the girl who had come as governess to Mr. Meadows' was the daughter of an osteopath in London. 'Yes,' said he, 'I'll go to Hanover if thur yunt some farriners a-getting up in London nowadays. Was he on our side or the Kaiser's in the war?' I didn't try to explain. It would have been a pity. Stocky was getting old now but he could still shoot. 'I a just shot a rabbit,' he said. 'Too close. I blowed his yud all of a mommy' (to pomace, pulp).

This change-over to vegetable growing meant a lot of heavy land was either sown down to grass from arable or, as Tom said, 'fell down', to become turf by grazing and mowing and some basic slag sown by hand broadcast. This slag sowing was a filthy job and the fine particles got on the chest and caused bronchitis. This killed one of the Bradfields. Dr. Overthrow said that had

Bradfield drunk plenty of cider while slag sowing, he would have lived. The doctor, though unorthodox, had lived his life in the country and, as it were, kept his ear close to the ground, preferring his own ideas to modern medicine. He died at a great age.

Dad's and Mr. Carter's methods wouldn't do today but they made an impact on this village. Mr. Carter was hardly ever without his gun and planted parsley on Bredon Hill to attract the hares. He had an eye like a hawk and I have never seen rabbits bowled over running as he did it, with his twelve-bore gun inches in front of his dog's nose. I lost his best fitcher ferret deep in a holt in Clay Furlong. 'Never mind, boy, you'll learn,' he said. 'You cut the line, I suppose.' I had to admit I did. 'Don't forget to tell your Dad what a hard day's rabbiting we've had today,' he said. I didn't. We had been digging in rock but we had a good bag. Just lately it has dawned on me why Mr. Carter liked my company. He hadn't a son of his own.

Dad bought a patch of Lincoln peas at Frogmore near Moreton and was told of some for sale at Bourton-on-the-Hill. He showed me the farm but the farmer was out that day. Next day Mr. Carter said he would go and make a deal for these peas. 'You come with me, Fred. You know where it is.' He used to take me out quite a bit in his car. At two o'clock he called for me. He was dressed in his grey tweed breeches, cloth buttoned-up leggings, his market jacket and trilby. He looked smart, a man mellowed with age. 'Get in the front by me.' His two dogs were in the back. I was thrilled to have such an afternoon away from Walt and the horses. As we drove and farmed as we went it was an experience. There was little traffic. 'I don't like the look of Frank Hedge's sprouts,' he said as we took the Evesham road. 'What's the matter with them, Mr. Carter?' I humbly said. 'Just calling out for a bit a nitre. They're as blue as whetstone. They're gone hard (stopped growing). Nice covey a birds in the next field but one on the stubble,' he told me. We saw the lot, both sides of the road. Turning for Childswickham, we ran past a field where Mr. Carter recognised an old friend, Decimus Somebody. As the car stopped and we got out he said, 'If you want to see a nice piece of early gillies, come and look at Decimus's,' It was September and they almost met in the rows, bushes of promising wallflowers. 'Save me a bit of that seed next year,' Mr. Carter asked him, 'I'll remember, Harry, but I wouldn't let anybody have it. It's took me years to get it so early.' Going up Broadway Hill a sports car had the cheek to pass us. 'Was that a woman?' Mr. Carter asked me. I had to admit it was. 'You know, Fred, nobody used to pass me at one time. Now they fly past.' 'Dangerous bend,' I said. 'She should have stayed behind.' 'Ah, but that's not it,' he said. 'This car's been beat and I'm getting old.' The white hair under his trilby and his white moustache gave him an appearance I thought I wouldn't mind having one day. 'You were at Chapel on Sunday, Fred?' I said, 'Yes, why?' 'Well, it was the harvest and you remember the theme was "The Falling of the Leaf"?' I did. With a deep sigh he said, 'That's meant for me. I've had my day. Autumn has come and winter will soon be here with me.' 'You work too hard, both you and Dad,' I said. 'Why don't you take it steadier?' 'When I can't keep up with the rest of the men at any job, I'll finish,' he said.

We reached the pea-field and the farmer, Bob Jones, was having an after-dinner nap. As we walked through the field, the pods full of green fresh peas (Senators with no mildew), rabbits and hares were scurrying in all directions. The dogs were in the car. Bob Jones asked us into the cool slab-floored hall and he and Mr. Carter talked about everything under the sun—foxes, badgers, the government, the weather—never mentioning peas. Then, like a shot from his twelve-bore, Mr. Carter said, 'Well, what's the name of the child?' This was a bit of real Evesham bargaining. He meant, 'How much for the field of peas?' Bob Jones reckoned there were so many hundred pots. Mr. Carter's estimate was lower and eventually they decided to make a bargain at so much a pot when we picked them, rather than so much for the field. Mr. Carter told me on the way home that had he known there had been so much mud around Bob Jones's farm he would not have put his 'tea drinkers' on. I knew what he meant—his light boots. A bottle of pop and a lardy cake in

Broadway completed a pleasant afternoon.

The peas turned out well, but that was Mr. Carter's last pea-picking season. Next autumn he went, as he said he would, with the falling of the leaf.

The change in the pattern of life of both field and fireside was often so gradual that it wasn't noticed at the time. The thin end of the wedge describes it. The increase in market gardening in this edge of the Evesham Vale village brought with it a demand for a lighter-legged type of horse. The massive shire horses of the corn farms were too big and too slow for working the horse hoes up the sprout and pea rows and good half-legged nags were tailored for the job. Turning them on the headland at skim or horse hoe caused less damage. Handy nags stepped with their smaller hooves in between the plants. They also fitted the bill for horse rakes in the hay fields and taking the milk to the station on dray or float.

Syd Hungerford, who followed Mr. Meadows at Higford House, brought with him some real shire horses, the last young ones we saw in the village. Tom Wheatcroft told me he could raise a horse up from a screw (a bad doer). I remember one such pony he bought for a fiver in Gloucester market which, by his art and know-how, he made into the finest animal I ever saw go up our village, old Syd sitting in his tub, reins loose, apparently doing nothing. Syd carried certain herbs in his pockets. The smell attracted and he could catch any horse. His son tells me he kept the secret till his death.

But what of our horses (or Walt's)? They seem like old soldiers. They never die; they simply fade away. The day the tractor came, a Fordson with an Oliver plough, there was a sort of quietness among the old men which could almost be felt. Our clay ground had taken four horses on a single-furrow plough; this paraffin job pulled a two-furrow plough. That autumn Bert Wheatcroft, Tom's son, started ploughing where the peas and beans had been, and even the old shepherd admitted he was doing a fairish job. It was Tom this time who was dubious. The first field was finished and Walt ploughed the headlands with his four remaining horses. Tom said, 'I've sin some of this caper when I was at Meadows's place. Thee wait till we gets some rain.' Rain came and these being days before hydraulics, the Old Girl, as Bert called his tractor, dug herself in and Walt pulled him out with his ' 'osses' and the plough was left in the furrow. As the weeks passed and the field was waterlogged the tractor had a melancholy look in the barn. Bert had his leg pulled. 'When bist a gwain to finish ploughing the Thurness?' Walt said. 'Too wet,' said Bert. 'It'll pad the ground.' Tom came into the barn. 'Oi,' he said. 'I a-knowed the time when I was carter for old Freddy. I was only nineteen year old when we kept guntly (gently) on all the winter at plough, the winter a'mus (almost) half filling the furrows.' 'Did you get very wet?' I said. 'Bless the boy! A Midland Railway sack over yer shoulders, another round yer waist tied a bagging string and I'd say, "Send it down, David".' The rain, he'd meant. 'What I means,' he continued, 'we kept guntly on and thy contraption a bin in yer a fortnit tomorrow.' 'What about snow, Tom?' I said. 'Well, that's a bit different. Old Freddy'd never let ya plough snow in. It kept the ground cold all the spring.' Bert got going again when the weather took up and a good job he did.

Turpin, our foremost horse at plough, was always fond of apples and he went down with the gripes after breaking through into the Tythe Court Orchard and filling himself with Bramley seedlings. I had the unthankful task of walking him up and down the road and not letting him lie down. 'Half a turpentine and half a linsid oil', Tom drenched him with. He got a bit better after a few visits from the vet, but his teeth were going and he went, as Walt put it, 'as wake (weak) as a robbin'. I shed a tear when the knacker man shot him outside the Nag Stable and Old Shepherd said, 'I s'pose that's another to gu in Spaldings's meat and bone manure.' There is something sad about the end of a faithful horse. It's like the felling of some ancient tree that has given shelter from the storm and shade from the hot sun. Turpin was winched up on to the slaughterer's lorry, he who had been stabled in the loose box with the half door and, putting his head over, had craned his neck and watched me fetch him a skip or basket of bait, a mixture of chaff mangolds and oat flour from the granary and whinnied as I returned. 'It's no good thee a-snivelling, Fred,' said Walt. 'Sometimes young 'osses'll die. Old 'osses be bound to.'

Although Bert did the ploughing with the tractor, Walt still hauled the hay with the horses after Bert had cut the mowing grass, the local blacksmith converting the mowing machine so that the tractor could pull it with Walt on the mowing machine seat. The horses went as Turpin went, most of them completing their alloted span of about twenty-five to thirty years. I liked to go in Boss Close on a summer Sunday afternoon and watch the horses as they enjoyed their rest, rolling on the grass, sometimes lying stretched out in the sun. Bonnie I photographed as she got up front legs first and remained in a sitting position as if posing for me. She had been sold once for seventy guineas to pull a brewer's dray on the streets of Birmingham but returned lame after a week. She lived to thirty-two, outliving Turpin, her eldest son.

Joe Baker, one-time shepherd for John Bosworth and manager over Jasper, the ploughman there, just slipped away, aged nearly ninety, while I was on holiday one summer. He told me once how Jasper was ploughing Hempits. Joe was nearly half a mile away on Paris Hill with his sheep. Noticing one of Jasper's team pulling askew he thought, I'll bet old Sharper's pinched (sore shoulders). 'Shutting off time,' he said, 'I went in the stable and there was the tell-tale raw bit on his shoulder about as big as a shilling. "Turn him up," I told Jasper, and rubbing some alum on the sore I ordered Jasper not to work him for a week.'

Funny how some can see from a distance what Jasper couldn't spot from the plough tails. Jasper has only just left this earthly scene, having spent his last few years with relatives at a South Coast resort. I'd have loved to have met him on the Promenade. He walked with a stick with a horse's-head handle. 'Won it at hoopla years ago at Dumbleton Flower Show.'

After the shepherd's death Walt looked after the sheep for a time. The time had come when we were left with two light-legged nags to horse-hoe the vegetable crops, Bert doing the rest with the tractor. Walt was a good carter but not an ideal shepherd. He just hadn't the approach. At our back door one night he came out with one of his classic examples of unconscious wit. 'Master, you'll have to come up along-a me on to the Leasow in the morning. Hughes's ewes and Hughie's ewes be got along with your ewes and there's a tup amongst um with long horns and he stinks like a billy-goat.' We went up in the morning. Our ewes were marked blue in the middle of the back and order was restored. Tom Wheatcroft and I took over after and we had a good lambing season but one or two of the lambs had horns, the result of the mix-up with the tup.

Tom Wheatcroft, who in his younger days could carry a two and a quarter hundredweight sack of wheat up anywhere, told me he had got that he could just about carry the empty sack. 'I was born too soon. That's my trouble,' he said when I went to see him in hospital before he died. He probably gave one of the best compliments anyone could give to the nursing profession. 'They be just like angels, Fred, how they have treated me.' I thought a bit and was satisfied that it was no more than he deserved.

Walt is still with us, bent and deaf but nimble for his eighty-five years. He told me the other day that there were only he and Arthur Bradfield and Tom Wheatcroft's brother left who could remember the Squire. 'I should still be all right to do a bit of work but it's my legs. I bin on um a good while. Nice for you to call. I be allus glad to see you.'

Every summer up till almost the time of his death in the 1950s Uncle Jim came and spent a few days in our village, bringing with him one of his many grandchildren. Towards the end, as he hobbled round our place as far as his gammy leg would allow, he would tell me of his old haunts. He'd been away for about sixty years but still could show me where to find the mushrooms in Wet Furrow, the early blackberries on the Lower Grave Hill, the nuts in the Primrose Coppice—in fact, we relived much which happened in the Squire's time. He took me to the thatched bull pen anent (or opposite) the cider mill, where the savage white shorthorn bull was kept.

Uncle Jim told me he was a great believer in the belt, adding, 'I always used to give my youngest lad a good hiding every Saturday dinner time and send him to bed. I hadn't got time in the wick.' He had a great sense of humour and when a young farmer asked him if he could marry his eldest granddaughter, Uncle Jim said, 'Yes, on one condition. That is you bring me a good load of muck for my allotment.'

CHAPTER TWENTY-SIX

CONCLUSIONS THROUGH A FARMHOUSE WINDOW

WHAT IS in store for our village under the hill? The prospects, I believe, are good. Some of the people, particularly the young couples, are bringing new ideas and I visualise a social life returning again.

The tendency just at the moment is to get away in the car; 'whither shall we wander?' But already I can see signs of people staying at home, a return to the simple life of garden and fireside. Having tried everything, 'gone further and fared worse', 'found the crows as black elsewhere as here', they are ready for a slowing down of the tempo of life. This may be only a pipe dream, but you do hear people saying, 'I don't go on the roads Bank Holidays', or 'There's no pleasure in motoring today', that sort of thing. I notice newcomers walking for pleasure, though I'm afraid I must admit that a lot of the natives, like myself, walk only when we are obliged to—we did so much walking in the past.

Villages like ours, when the system of motorways has been extended, will be little oases where the visitor can see a bit of old England. The characters I have described here 'made a good staddle to build on', as Tom Wheatcroft would have put it. They knew their Ayshon (Ashton). They loved it. They studied it. If you asked them the way to Campden, they possibly could not have told you. But they knew the Rabbit Lane at Beckford where Spring-Heeled Jack was supposed to meet the White Lady on moonlight nights. They talked of Bobbity Lantern's 'Will o' the Wisps' in the Dewrest by Carrants Brook. Or the Cuckoo Pen on Little Hill. This group of trees still stands. I wonder whether Squire Bosworth had anything to do with this? You see, the old idea of penning the cuckoo was that by keeping him enclosed all winter and not letting him return to southern lands, they could keep with him a state of perpetual spring and summer.

It has often been said that when we look back over the years the pleasant things are what we remember most. My youth was full of a sense of security. Nothing seemed to change. Mrs. Hill trimmed and filled our oil lamps every morning, cleaned the candlesticks and replaced burnt-out candles. The corner cupboard in the kitchen (used as a medicine store) contained castor oil, goose grease, camphorated oil, eucalyptus, iodine, linseed and liquorice. There was also sulphur for making brimstone and treacle, and permanganate of potash used for a multitude of purposes, from gargling to colouring the staircase. Dad whitewashed our kitchen ceiling using lime size and blue bag and shouted up the stairs the next morning, 'It's as yellow as a guinea. I shall have to do it again.' Another thing kept in the medicine cupboard in a blue bottle marked 'poison' was carbolic acid. During 'flu epidemics Dad took a shovelful of red-hot embers off the fire in our old oven grate and dropped spots of carbolic over them while he walked around the house blowing the fumes into every crook and cranny upstairs and downstairs. I have never seen anyone else do this. As I look back, the clearer it becomes to me that he put a lot of time and thought into our welfare.

We always had a fish tea on Fridays. Dad bought some from Allan Harding at Evesham, who had a stall under the town hall and bought our rabbits.

Next to the tea caddy on our mantelpiece was an old tin which belonged to Dad's grandfather. It contained black and white striped humbugs. Grandfather was Liberal and Chapel but Great-Grandfather was Tory. Dad told me that when he was a small boy Great-Grandfather said to him, 'What are you, Tommy?' 'True Blue,' Dad told him and then he had a humbug. Bribery and corruption, you may say, but really just a bit of fun.

This summer I have met some people from Newcastle-on-Tyne. Naturally those who live up north enjoy the change of

scenery of the Cotswold country, the Vale of Evesham, Tewkesbury and its abbey, Stratford-upon-Avon and Shakespeare's
birthplace. One man said to me, 'What I like about this district
is that there's a village about every three miles and all different.'
Some of them thought us a bit modest and suggested that by
giving the history of old houses on plaques, the tourist could
sum up a village more readily. We want tourists to visit our
beauty spots, not to go through at sixty miles an hour. If our
villages are to be, not exactly show places, but places to visit,
study and photograph, certainly it's our business to know as
much as we can about them. It's pathetic how little people
nowadays know of where they live. The driver of a car stopped
the other day and asked a friend of mine about our village cross.
He's lived here thirty years. He told the motorist it was a
memorial to the men who were killed in the Boer War. 'I was
right, wasn't I?' he asked. 'No, it's fifteenth century,' I told
him. 'You should have known,' I added.

'Where is everybody?' one Tynesider said to me one day.
'They are working at all points of the compass,' I answered.
'They'll be home for tea.' 'Shall I meet them in the local?' he
said. 'Some, but others will be off again in their cars to town,' I
replied. From the time when I was a small boy until just about a
year ago, I knew everybody who lived in our village. A point has
been reached when that's no longer possible. The population has
increased, but not a great deal. Yet so many only sleep here. It is
a blessing that the local industries have absorbed the labour of
our villages to such an extent, but a pity that once the youths
have seen the bright lights they go there for their entertainment.
It is my personal opinion that there is a need in our villages for
some sort of evening sessions (I won't say classes) for educa-
tional discussion, culture and local history blended with entertainment. The Women's Institutes are doing a good job in this
direction. Youth clubs are struggling. I find them more successful when they have connections with a church. The need is for
higher age groups among the men, who have too much tele-
vision and lack the opportunity of mixing. The young meet their

girl-friends. I must say that in our village standards are good and the majority know how to behave. But the old adage still is very true,

> 'A sigh too much, or a kiss too long,
> And there follows a mist and a weeping rain,
> And life is never the same again.'

Last night I took a walk around some of my old haunts. The Little Piece where we slid in winter on the big pond is now the sports field. Cricket thrives—I'm so glad. Tennis—the courts are not used to the full. There are iron-framed swings with strong chains for the children. I came back and looked at the old cider apple tree in the orchard where we swung from a waggon rope, the wooden seat a plank bored by Oliver's auger. The tree, I remember, once bore a ton of fruit.

Although the roads are maintained by the Council we have lost our roadman. I'm sorry. He knew every drain and path in our parish and gritted the slippery road corners before a lot of folk were up on frosty mornings. No longer do we hear the ring of his whetstone as he sharpens his scythe. The mowing is done by the Council. No complaints, except for the loss of the personal touch. Tractors can't do some of the awkward slopes Arthur Bradfield did.

By now you will have realised that I have been mainly content with the pleasure of home, but it's good to return from a holiday to the old fireside with a fresh store of memories and ideas. Emerson says, 'The domestic man who loves no music so well as his own kitchen clock and the airs which the logs sing to him as they burn on the hearth has solaces which others never dream of.' It is so true that when we retire into ourselves we can call up what memories we please.

Take a moonlit walk in an unlit village street and watch the moon just as it has risen from behind the Cotswold Hills journey slowly across the autumn sky. I have never wondered at those who worshipped the sun or the moon.

In the raw mid-winter when

> 'Outside fall the snowflakes lightly
> Through the night loud raves the storm.
> In my room the fire glows brightly
> And 'tis cosy, silent, warm;
> Musing sit I on the settle
> By the firelight's cheerful blaze,
> Listening to the busy kettle,
> Humming long forgotten lays.'

These are the nights to get into a book, the wind outside stirring the doors of the old house and adding a little to the enjoyment as we travel without leaving our fireside. These, indeed, are perfect moments of life on earth.